rebecca robb benne
jon hird

move

advanced

coursebook
with CD-ROM

MACMILLAN

move advanced contents map

Module 1 Individuals

Module 2 Pairs

Module 3 Groups

Unit	Topic	Language study	Vocabulary	Main skills
1 **Living together** pages 66–69	• Happy families (Britain's biggest family) • A social experiment (living in an alternative community)	• Ellipsis and substitution	• Family relationships • Community organisation	• **Reading:** understanding gist; understanding vocabulary in context • **Speaking:** discussing cultural values and family relationships; discussing the aims of non-traditional living communities • **Listening:** identifying key information • **Writing:** an online advert
2 **Talk talk** pages 70–73	• World languages (Are fewer languages better?) • Language learning (attitudes to learning English and other foreign languages)	• Forming adjectives from verbs and nouns (adjective suffixes)	• Sensitive language (euphemisms)	• **Reading:** predicting; understanding main information and vocabulary in context • **Speaking:** evaluating the cultural and practical value of languages; using sensitive language and softeners to avoid offence • **Listening:** identifying key information • **Pronunciation:** sentence stress
3 **Net value** pages 74–77	• Is the Internet a good thing? • Are you addicted to email? (survey report)	• Using vague language	• Phrasal verbs: communication • Surveys	• **Listening:** understanding gist and key information; understanding vocabulary in context • **Speaking:** discussing the Internet; clarifying information and checking understanding; talking about email addiction; conducting a survey • **Pronunciation:** stress and weak forms • **Reading:** understanding key information • **Writing:** a survey report
4 **Team spirit** pages 78–81	• Team building • Are you a team player?	• Dependent prepositions	• World of work	• **Reading:** predicting information; checking key information and vocabulary in context • **Speaking:** discussing work practices and leadership styles; describing college- or work-related problems and giving advice • **Listening:** identifying key information; understanding vocabulary in context • **Writing:** a programme script

5 **Review unit** pages 82–85
- **Extra practice** pages 86–89 • **Grammar reference and wordlist** pages 90–92 • **Listening scripts** pages 94–95 • **Communication activities** pages 93, 96
- **Use CD2 for listening activities in this module.**

CD-ROM

Location	• Modules 1–3
Activities for each unit	• Language activity • Vocabulary activity • Common European Framework linked activity • Language game
Features	• Markbook – helps you to record and update your marks. • Bookmark – helps you to save your favourite activities. • Wordlist – helps you to create your own wordlists. • You can back up, restore and print out your Markbook, Bookmarks and Wordlists. You can also send saved files as emails. • For more information use the Help feature.

move advanced at a glance

In the Coursebook:

three 32-page modules

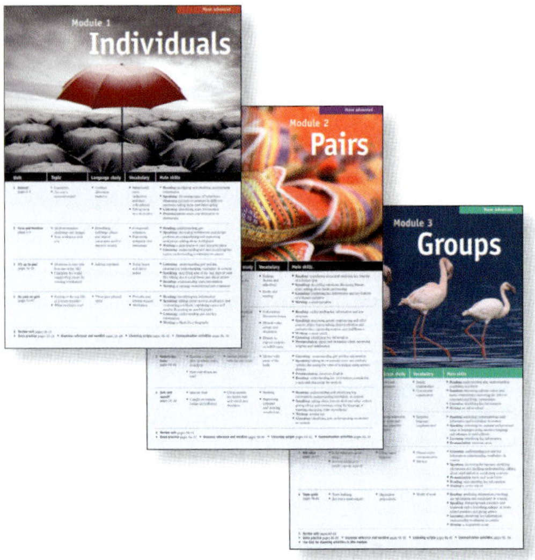

On the CD-ROM:

48 language activities and games, a help section and markbook, wordlist and bookmark features

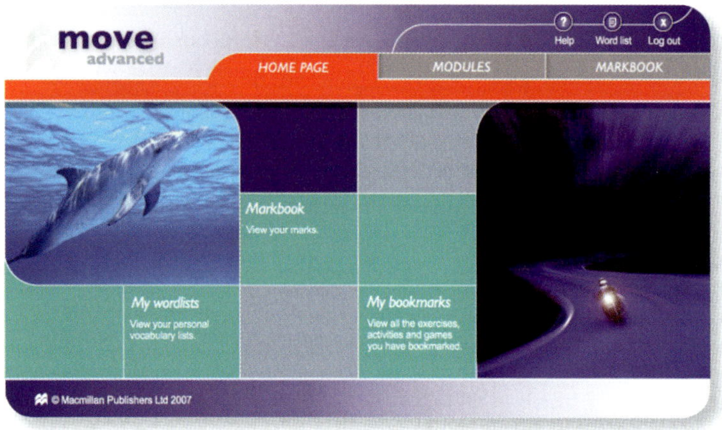

In each module:

four main units

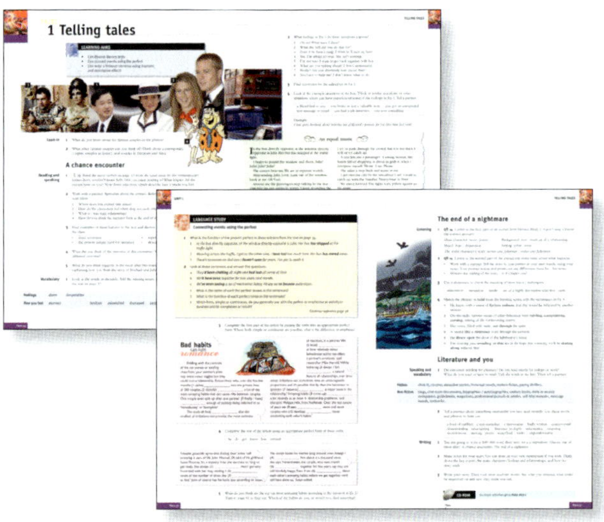

a review unit

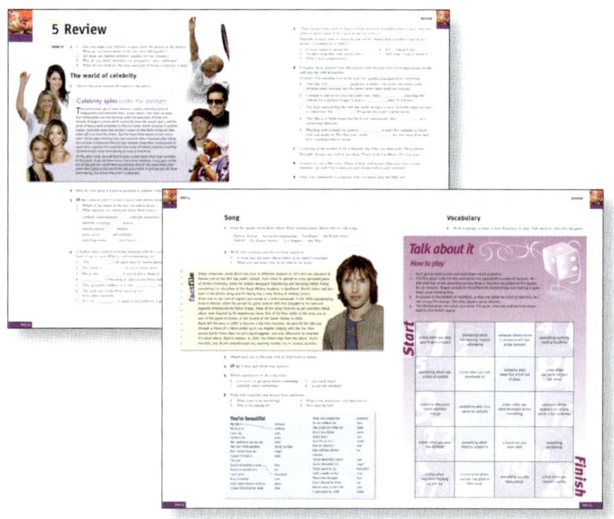

four extra practice pages

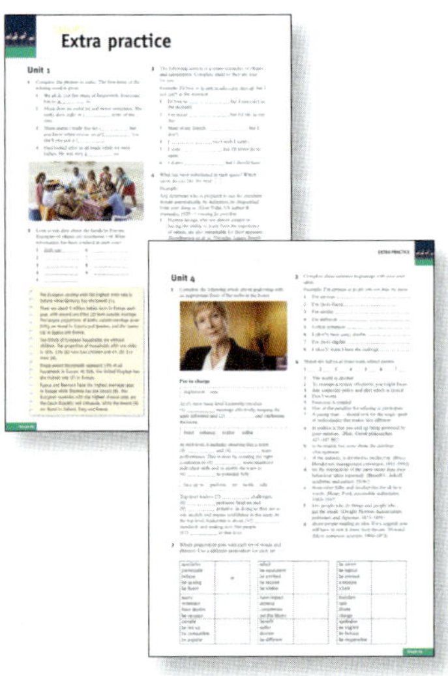

five reference pages: grammar, wordlist and listening scripts

two communication activity pages

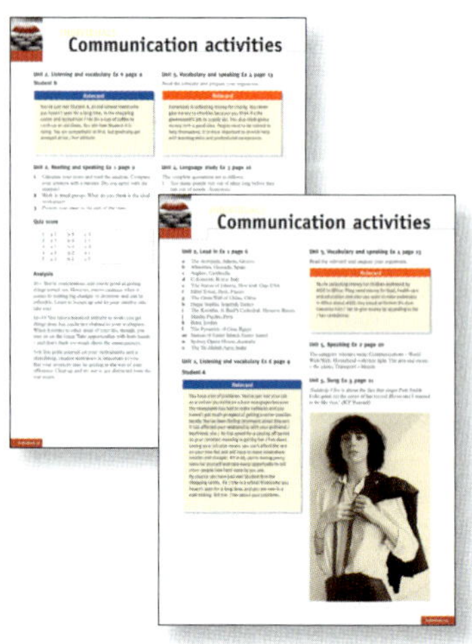

Module 1
Individuals

Unit	Topic	Language study	Vocabulary	Main skills
1 **Behave!** pages 2–5	• Eccentrics • Are you a nonconformist?	• Contrast (discourse markers)	• Behavioural traits (adjectives and their collocations) • Taking turns in a discussion	• **Reading:** predicting and checking; summarising information • **Speaking:** discussing types of behaviour; discussing pressure to conform in different countries; taking turns and interrupting • **Listening:** identifying main information • **Pronunciation:** stress and intonation in discussions
2 **Form and function** pages 6–9	• Modern wonders (buildings and design) • Your workspace and you	• Describing buildings, places and objects (structures used to describe nouns)	• Compound adjectives • Expressing sympathy and annoyance	• **Reading:** understanding gist • **Speaking:** discussing architecture and design preferences; sympathising and expressing annoyance; talking about workspaces • **Writing:** a description of your favourite place • **Listening:** understanding gist and identifying key topics; understanding vocabulary in context
3 **It's up to you!** pages 10–13	• Moments in time (the best day of my life) • Changing the world (supporting causes by wearing wristbands)	• Adding emphasis	• Social issues and direct action	• **Listening:** understanding gist and key information; understanding vocabulary in context • **Speaking:** describing one of the best days of your life; talking about social issues and direct action • **Reading:** understanding main information • **Writing:** a message board thread and comments
4 **No pain, no gain** pages 14–17	• Getting to the top (life of a sumo wrestler) • What motivates you?	• Three-part phrasal verbs	• Proverbs and idioms: success • Motivation	• **Reading:** identifying key information • **Speaking:** talking about success, motivation and overcoming problems; explaining causes and results; discussing an autobiography • **Listening:** understanding gist and key information • **Writing:** a blurb for a biography

5 **Review unit** pages 18–21

• **Extra practice** pages 22–25 • **Grammar reference and wordlist** pages 26–28 • **Listening scripts** pages 30–31 • **Communication activities** pages 29, 32

1 Behave!

LEARNING AIMS

- Can use discourse markers to contrast information
- Can discuss types of behaviour
- Can take turns in a discussion

Eccentrics

Lead-in

1 Work in groups. Which of the people in the box are in the photos? What do you know about these six people? What is / was strange or different about them?

Björk	Salvador Dalí	Albert Einstein
Frida Kahlo	Ozzy Osbourne	Vincent van Gogh

2 There are many famous male eccentrics, but few female. Why do you think this is so?

3 Read this quote by American author Michael J. Gelb. Do you agree?

Crazy people who are productive are geniuses.
Crazy people who are rich are eccentric.
Crazy people who are neither productive nor rich are just plain crazy.

Reading

1 Do you think these statements are true or false? Discuss them with a partner.

1 Eccentrics are generally optimistic and interested in finding out things.
2 Most eccentrics don't mind being made fun of.
3 Eccentricity is something which people have no control over.

2 **01** Read the magazine interview on page 3. Find the answers to Ex 1.

3 Is David Weeks positive or negative about eccentricity? Write a paragraph (60–80 words) and summarise his main results and opinions.

4 Compare your summaries with a partner. Have you included similar information?

5 Look at this scale from conformity (1) to individuality (5). Where are you on the scale? Why? Explain this to a partner.

conformity ← 1 — 2 — 3 — 4 — 5 → individuality

Vocabulary and speaking

1 Look at these words from the text. Underline the main stressed syllable.

conventional curious gloomy intelligent mischievous opinionated rebellious unorthodox

2 **02** Listen and check your answers.

3 Work with a partner. Agree which words in Ex 1 have positive meanings and which have negative meanings. Think of words with similar and opposite meanings.

4 Tell a partner which of the adjectives in Ex 1–3 apply to you. Explain why or give examples of specific situations.

Example:
I am quite opinionated. I have very strong opinions about things like religion and politics, and I often get into arguments about them.

5 Complete these sentences with the words in the box to make collocations. Check your answers in the text.

collector imagination outlook side traits

1 Anna has a vivid _________.
2 Tom is an obsessive _________.
3 Jack's got a strong creative _________.
4 Sara's got a few eccentric _________.
5 Rick has an optimistic _________ on life.

6 Replace the names in Ex 5 with the names of people you know. Work with a partner and tell your partner about these people.

7 Which of these adjectives can be used with which nouns in Ex 5? Do you know any other nouns which collocate with these words? Example: *avid collector*

avid dark fertile feminine gloomy keen overactive positive serious sympathetic unconventional

An interview with David Weeks, author of *Eccentrics, a study of sanity and strangeness*

According to David Weeks, eccentrics like Mr Christmas 'don't give a damn what the rest of the world thinks of them'. Mr Christmas (real name Andy Park) has celebrated Christmas with Christmas dinner and presents every day for twelve years.

Happy, healthy and *odd!*

Q: **What prompted you to make a scientific study of eccentricity?**
A: Psychologists have undertaken exhaustive studies of every personality type under the sun, yet somehow we have completely overlooked eccentrics. And psychiatry, on the other hand, tends only to take an interest in those who seek treatment, and since eccentrics rarely do so, they have been overlooked. I thought it might contribute something important to our understanding of the mind if we had a better understanding of the thought processes of those who regard themselves and who are regarded by others as eccentric.

Q: **Can you give us a description of the eccentric?**
A: The eccentric is very creative and curious and has vivid visual imagination in the daytime and vivid dreams at night. Eccentrics are intelligent, opinionated, and frequently have a mischievous sense of humour. Many of them are loners, and they often have unorthodox living arrangements.

Q: **For example?**
A: We have several men who lived in caves. Women eccentrics tend to be obsessive collectors and renovators. One woman in our study has 7,500 garden gnomes on her lawn.

Q: **You found in your study that eccentrics are happier and healthier than the rest of us.**
A: We did meet a few gloomy eccentrics, but most of the subjects in our study had a refreshingly sunny outlook on life. There is also pretty solid proof that eccentrics are healthier than the norm. In Great Britain the average person goes to the doctor twice a year, while eccentrics will typically go for eight or nine years without seeking medical help. It's not that they're avoiding doctors or don't believe in conventional medicine. They just don't need it much.

Q: **How do you explain this?**
A: It's a combination of an optimistic outlook and low stress, due to the fact that eccentrics don't feel the need to conform. Eccentrics don't give a damn what the rest of the world thinks of them; if someone makes fun of them, instead of getting angry or embarrassed, they regard the other person as the one with a problem.

Q: **What makes a person an eccentric? After all, everyone has some unusual habits or traits.**
A: Eccentricity is a choice. It's quite true that everyone has eccentric traits, but as we grow older, most of us learn to conform, to blend in – the process we call socialisation. But the eccentric says, 'No, thank you,' and chooses not to conform.

Q: **Are men or women more likely to be eccentric?**
A: The incidence of eccentricity is about the same, but it manifests itself in different ways. Society has always been more tolerant of aberrant behaviour in men than in women. If a man gets into a fight with a colleague or goes off on a drinking spree, we might overlook it, but if a woman does the same thing it's considered scandalous. A woman sometimes becomes eccentric later in life: she conforms in her youth, marries and has children, but once the kids have left home, she leaves her husband and lets her eccentric, creative side take over.

Q: **Dr Weeks, are you eccentric?**
A: I would say that I may have always been slightly eccentric, perhaps a little rebellious. I do, however, admire the authentic, life-long eccentrics. I think we can all learn a lot from them about holding onto the dreams and curiosity we had as children.

LANGUAGE STUDY

Contrast

1 Underline the four other contrastive discourse markers in these sentences.

a *Psychologists have studied every personality type, yet somehow we have overlooked eccentrics. And psychiatry, on the other hand, tends only to take an interest in those who seek treatment.*

b *We did meet a few gloomy eccentrics, but most of the subjects had a refreshingly sunny outlook on life.*

c *In Great Britain the average person goes to the doctor twice a year, while eccentrics will typically go for eight or nine years without seeking medical help.*

d *I would say that I may have always been slightly eccentric, perhaps a little rebellious. I do, however, admire the authentic, life-long eccentrics.*

2 Contrastive discourse markers most commonly go between the ideas they are contrasting, but there are other possible positions. Complete the table with the discourse markers from Ex 1.

Must always go between the ideas they are contrasting	Can also go before the first idea they are contrasting	Can also go in various positions in the second sentence
________ ________	even though whereas ________	nevertheless ________ ________

3 What is the function of the verb *do* in sentences 'b' and 'd'?

Grammar reference page 26

4 Look at these biography extracts. Combine each sentence 1–5 with one of the sentences a–e in **two** different ways using appropriate discourse markers.

Example:
Van Gogh was a truly great artist, ***yet*** *he only sold one painting in his lifetime.*
Even though *Van Gogh was a truly great artist, he only sold one painting in his lifetime.*

1 David Bowie has created some of the most colourful personas in popular music.
2 The young Einstein couldn't read or write until he was eight years old.
3 Most people get into the music business to actively seek fame and fortune.
4 At school Gaudí did rather badly in most subjects.
5 Dalí based his appearance on the fashion style of a century earlier.

a *Nirvana* front man Kurt Cobain found the invasion of his privacy all too much.
b His paintings were anything but retrospective.
c He has been virtually colour blind since a childhood accident.
d He went on to become perhaps the greatest scientist of the 20th century.
e He did excel in geometry, which inspired his lifetime's work.

5 Join the two sentences using *but* and the auxiliary verb *do* to emphasise contrast.

Example: I enjoyed the meal. The service wasn't too good.
I did enjoy the meal, but the service wasn't too good.

1 I wanted to go. It was just impossible.
2 I like them. I've just listened to them too much.
3 I enjoyed it. I was glad to get home.
4 I agree I should do it more. Sometimes I just can't be bothered.
5 We liked each other. It just wasn't to be.
6 I felt for them. There was nothing I could do to help.

6 Work with a partner. Explain situations in your life to which some of the sentences in Ex 5 could apply.

Example: *I went to that new café near the school yesterday. I did enjoy the meal, but the service was a bit slow.*

Are you a nonconformist?

Listening and speaking

1 Discuss and agree on a definition of a nonconformist.

2 **03** Listen to the classroom discussion about nonconformists. Explain these statements by Alex, Mette and Natsuko talking about their country.

3 Discuss the opinions in Ex 2 in groups. Are any of these things true about your country? How much pressure is there to conform in your country in terms of dress, behaviour and lifestyle?

Vocabulary and pronunciation

Taking turns in a discussion

1 Listen again. Pay attention to stress and intonation, and write the phrases used when …

1. Alex takes up his point after interruption by Mette. *Er, yeah …*
2. Mette interrupts Alex the second time. *That …*
3. Natsuko interrupts Mette. *Sorry …*
4. Natsuko prevents Mette from interrupting. *Wait …*
5. Natsuko prevents Alex interrupting. *Just …*
6. Mette takes up an earlier point again. *To get …*

2 Put the phrases from Ex 1 in the correct place in the table. Then work with a partner and add the phrases in the box to the table.

Before you comment, can I just … By the way … Can I add something?
Can I finish what I was saying? Hang on! Incidentally … Where was I?

Interrupting	Preventing interruption	Returning to a topic	Changing the topic
		Er, yeah … Anyway,	

Speaking

1 Work in groups. Look at the discussion circle and add two topics of your own.

1 We will all end up following in our parents' footsteps.

2 ______________________

3 Uniforms (at school and at work) infringe people's right to express their individuality.

4 ______________________

5 It's better to live in an anonymous city than in a close-knit village.

2 Working individually, note down two arguments for and against each topic.

3 Your group has ten minutes to discuss all the topics. Start by discussing topic 1. Then in turns, change the topic to the next one in the circle until you return to the first topic.

CD-ROM For more activities go to **Individuals Unit 1**

2 Form and function

LEARNING AIMS

- Can describe buildings, places and objects
- Can talk about workspaces
- Can sympathise with problems

Modern wonders

Lead-in

1 These photos were on a shortlist for a competition to find the New Seven Wonders of the World. Do you know the names of the buildings and monuments? Or do you know where they are? (You can check with the list on page 29.)

2 What makes a building or monument a modern wonder? Discuss your ideas with the class, and make a list of your criteria.

3 Work in groups. Use the shortlist and agree on your New Seven Wonders of the World.

Reading and speaking

1 Work in groups. Look at the adjectives in the box and add other adjectives that can describe a building.

functional	modern	19th century	three-storey	smart	well-maintained

2 Think about the building where you have your English classes and discuss these questions.
1. What is it like inside? Is it a good environment for learning English?
2. What's the building like outside?

3 **04** Read the article on page 7. Does the author like the building? Why / Why not?

4 Answer these questions.
1. What's the official name of the building? What's its nickname and why?
2. What other metaphors have been used to describe it? Looking at the photo, which do you think is the most appropriate?
3. What do people in London think of it?
4. What special features does the building have?

5 Work in groups and discuss these statements.
1. Ultramodern buildings should not be built next to old buildings.
2. A company's building says a lot about the company itself.

A brilliant new skyscraper

At just 180 metres and 40 stories, the new skyscraper officially known as 30 St. Mary Axe is less than half the height of the world's ten tallest buildings, and not even the tallest building in London. But it draws instant attention because of its unique shape, which has been variously compared to a cigar, a rocket, a bullet, a lipstick, a Zeppelin airship, a lava lamp, a bandaged finger, and – most frequently – a gherkin. Its architect, Norman Foster, prefers the metaphor of a pine cone or pineapple, since they do more justice to the building's shape.

The Gherkin has rapidly become a well-known contemporary icon and much-loved tourist attraction. Most Londoners appreciate the novelty and sophistication of the building. Some despise it for desecrating the ancient City of London; but the quaint character of the City was pretty well desecrated decades ago by uninspired postwar rebuilding. The shape is a bit frivolous-looking for a building whose original owner was Swiss Re, a sober and respectable Zurich-based insurance company. But the sparkling glass surfaces covering the entire outside (made of 5,500 triangular windows, many of which open) and calm gray* walls inside the building are ultrachic and ultramodern.

The building is round in floor plan to reduce the high winds generated at street level by tall rectangular buildings. On each of the office levels (floors 2–34), six pie-shaped pieces have been cut out from the plan, with elevators* and other service facilities at the center*. These six open cuts allow natural daylight to penetrate far back towards the elevator core and add desirable window-facing working space.

Swiss Re is seriously concerned about the possible financial costs to its clients of such things as global warming, and was determined to make its London headquarters a model of environment-friendly, energy-saving design. Genuine fresh air from outside can be guided about and used to reduce the need for mechanical air conditioning. In the basement there are no spaces for cars, but there are racks for bicycles and showers for cyclists.

London's new symbol is a sparkling, sensuous but profoundly sensible tower.

Glossary
*gray, elevator, center = American English for 'grey', 'lift' and 'centre'

Vocabulary

1 Look at these compound adjectives from the text. What do they describe in the article, and what do they mean?

1 well-known
2 much-loved
3 frivolous-looking
4 Zurich-based
5 pie-shaped
6 window-facing
7 environment-friendly
8 energy-saving

2 Look at these compound adjectives. Which compound adjective in each set is not a correct collocation? What things could the other two words in each set describe?

Example:
best-known *singer in the world*   little-known *area*   terribly known *X*

1 well-loved   badly loved   much-loved
2 rainy-looking   expensive-looking   tasty-looking
3 American-based   London-based   Britain-based
4 sky-shaped   heart-shaped   crescent-shaped
5 south-facing   sea-facing   room-facing
6 world-friendly   child-friendly   tourist-friendly
7 time-saving   food-saving   money-saving

> **NOTE**
> Most compound adjectives have hyphens when they come before the noun, but when the first word ends in *-ly* there is no hyphen.
> Examples:
> Well-known,
> badly dressed

3 What other *-looking* compounds can you think of?

4 Rewrite these sentences using compound adjectives.

Example: I live in that building *with the bright colour* next to the market.
I live in that brightly coloured building next to the market.

1 That building *really catches your eye.*
2 I rent a flat *on the third floor.*
3 It's a flat *where you can't smoke.*
4 I have a flat *with two bedrooms.*
5 The cupboards *were made badly* and don't open properly.
6 There's a good café nearby where you can get a great breakfast *all day.*

5 Describe the place where you live to a partner. Use at least three compound adjectives.

Example: *I live in a three-roomed flat in an old four-storey building. The building has an elegant-looking entrance and beautiful windows. Our flat has a small south-facing balcony…*

LANGUAGE STUDY

Describing buildings, places and objects

1 Look at these extracts from the text on page 7 and the structures that describe the nouns in **bold**. Find other examples in the extracts.

1 adjectives *unique*
2 nouns used as adjectives *tourist*
3 relative clauses *which has been variously compared to a cigar, a rocket ...*
4 clauses beginning with a present (*-ing*) or past participle *covering the entire outside ...*
5 phrases beginning with a preposition *inside the building ...*

a *But it draws instant attention because of its unique **shape**, which has been variously compared to a cigar, a rocket ...*
b *The Gherkin has rapidly become a well-known contemporary **icon** and much-loved tourist **attraction**.*
c *The shape is a bit frivolous-looking for a **building** whose original owner was Swiss Re.*
d *But the sparkling glass **surfaces** covering the entire outside and calm gray **walls** inside the building are ultrachic and ultramodern.*
e *The building is round in floor **plan** to reduce the high **winds** generated at street level.*
f *Genuine fresh **air** from outside can be guided about.*

2 Which of the structures in Ex 1 go before the noun and which go after the noun?

Grammar reference page 27

3 Use one word or phrase from each column to describe four of the buildings and monuments from page 6.

Example:
It's a redbrick cathedral with multi-coloured domes standing in Red Square in Moscow.

	~~redbrick~~	pyramid	of a woman	~~standing in Red Square~~	in Egypt
	ruined	statue	discovered in 1908	at the entrance to the harbour	in Peru
It's a	4,500-year-old	city	made of two million blocks of stone	perched high in the Andes plateau	~~in Moscow~~
	copper	~~cathedral~~	~~with multi-coloured domes~~	rising 150 metres out of the desert	in New York

4 Complete the descriptions of the nouns in **bold** by adding the words and phrases in *italics* in the most natural order.

1 My favourite place to eat is a **restaurant**.
family-run *just round the corner from my house* *pizza* *called Luigi's*

2 My favourite item of clothing is a **jacket**.
with a hole in the sleeve *I've had since I was in my teens* *old* *denim* *faded*

3 My favourite film is *No way out*. It's a **thriller**.
starring Kevin Costner *with a great twist at the end* *fast-paced*

4 My favourite place anywhere in the world is Pushkar in India. It's a **town**.
with over 400 temples *chilled-out* *surrounding a holy lake* *small*

5 Adapt the sentences in Ex 4 to talk about your favourite place, etc.

Writing

1 Look at the competition and write your entry.

2 Read other students' entries. Which of the other places sound particularly interesting? Why? Choose the competition winner.

COMPETITION

Tell us about your favourite place in the world and win an all-expenses paid weekend in New York. Write about 200 words describing your favourite city, town, area or building and say why it is special to you.

Your workspace and you

Listening and vocabulary

1 Do you enjoy studying or working at home? What are the advantages and disadvantages?

2 05 Listen to the conversation and tick the things that Kyle talks about.

work and free time ☐ his business ☐ work colleagues ☐ girlfriends ☐
his social life ☐ office politics ☐ technical problems ☐ communication ☐
commuting ☐ independence ☐

3 Is Kyle positive or negative about working from home? Why?

4 Match Kyle's sentence beginnings to the endings. Underline the words that express dissatisfaction or annoyance.

1 I'm getting a bit sick	with being on my own.
2 I don't even have time to have lunch	it's driving me mad.
3 I miss	of sitting at my desk every day.
4 I'm fed up	let alone watch TV.
5 I get a new email every ten minutes and	the drinks after work with the lads.

5 Put these phrases into two lists: *sympathising* and *expressing annoyance*.

> Come on, it can't be that bad. Stop moaning! Oh, just shut up! Oh, poor you!
> What a shame! Oh, dear, I'm sorry. Oh, change the record! Put a sock in it!
> How awful! You're not the only one with problems, you know. Cheer up!

6 Listen to the conversation again and tick the phrases in Ex 5 that Nicola uses. Pay attention to stress and intonation.

7 Work with a partner. Student A look at page 29. Student B look at page 32. Review the phrases in this section for expressing dissatisfaction, sympathy and annoyance before you begin.

Reading and speaking

1 Complete the questionnaire. Then follow the instructions on page 32.

What does your workspace say about you?

1 How tidy is your workspace?
- a It's overflowing with all sorts of stuff.
- b There isn't a paperclip out of place.
- c You can usually find most things (fingers crossed!)

2 What about the personal items (photos, cuddly toys, magazines, etc) in your workspace?
- a What personal items? Your desk is for work, not fun.
- b There aren't many – you adhere to the minimalist approach.
- c They'd fill a small removal van.

3 How do you keep track of your appointments?
- a Make a mental note and hope it doesn't slip your mind.
- b Enter them in your computer calendar or diary as soon as they're scheduled.
- c Stick a post-it on your computer monitor, along with all the others.

4 Your computer wallpaper is …
- a an abstract pattern in soothing tones.
- b a motif from nature: a tropical beach, a lush forest, exotic flowers.
- c a picture of a universally-acclaimed member of the opposite sex.

5 You're feeling peckish while working, do you …
- a eat a piece of fruit from the bowl on your desk?
- b rummage through your desk drawer and hope something turns up?
- c have a snack away from your workspace to protect your keyboard from crumbs?

CD-ROM For more activities go to **Individuals Unit 2**

3 It's up to you!

LEARNING AIMS

- Can use emphasis when talking about important events
- Can discuss social issues and direct action
- Can contribute to message boards

▲ Martin Luther King

Moments in time

▲ Nelson Mandela

▲ Aung San Suu Kyi

▲ Gandhi

Lead-in

1 Work with a partner. Talk about what the people in the photos did to earn a place in the world's history books. Use the words in the box to help you.

apartheid	civil rights movement	democratic rule
equality	independence injustice	military rulers
non-violent protest	peace	segregation

Listening

1 **06** Listen to Jodie talking about one of the best days of her life. Make notes on these points.

The event: (What? Why? Where?) ____________________

____

Jodie's feelings at the start of the concert: (How did she feel? Why?) ____________________

____

____

How the concert changed Jodie's life: (What happened? How did her outlook on life change?) ____________________

____

____

____

2 Listen again and complete the words and phrases describing the feelings and reactions of Jodie and the crowd.

1. There was a great feeling, really ____________.
2. The crowd was ____________, but all the speeches rang a bit ____________ to me somehow.
3. The mood in the crowd seemed to ____________. There was this fantastic ____________.
4. It was like everyone's hope ____________ in this one man.
5. It was an absolute ____________ to me then, at that moment in time.
6. That day was a huge ____________ in my life.

3 Explain what the words and phrases in Ex 2 mean in this context.

Speaking

1 Think about these situations and make notes if necessary. Then tell your partner.

1. A time when you were in a crowd at a special event. What was the event? What was the mood? Did you feel part of the crowd or apart from it?
2. A revelation or turning point in your life. What led up to it? What happened? What were the consequences?

2 Discuss these questions with your class.

1. Is music a good way to create interest in a problem or raise money? What other ways can you think of drawing attention to a good cause or of raising money to help other people?
2. Do you think Bob Geldof will / should take a place in history in the same way as the people in the photos on this page? Think of arguments for and against.

LANGUAGE STUDY

Adding emphasis

1 Look at these extracts from Listening Ex 1–2 on page 10. Which include examples of:

1 adding emphasis to a noun? [*a*] [ ]
2 adding emphasis to an adjective? [ ] [ ]
3 adding emphasis to a verb or verb clause? [ ]
4 using a phrase to add emphasis to what you are saying in general? [ ]

a *The sun was blazing down and this* ***vast*** *crowd of people was chilling out.*
b *It was as if anything was possible, that music really could change the world,* ***you know.***
c *I* ***just*** *realised that my own experiences were so trivial.*
d *It's probably* ***even*** *harder to understand what it was like if you weren't there.*
e *It was an* ***absolute*** *revelation to me then, at that moment in time.*
f *This was a* ***very*** *special day.*

Grammar reference page 27

2 Match the words in **bold** to functions 1–4 in Ex 1.

a It's (1) **without doubt** the most amazing place I've (2) **ever** been to.
b The (3) **entire** event was a (4) **complete** waste of time.
c It was (5) **so** peaceful. We didn't see a (6) **single** person (7) **at all**.
d The house was (8) **absolutely** immaculate (9) **from top to bottom**. It was (10) **totally** spotless.

3 Put the words in *italics* in an appropriate position in the sentence to add emphasis.

Example: We didn't want the day to end. *just* *you know*
We just didn't want the day to end, you know.

1 I couldn't believe it. I was speechless. *just* *totally*
2 It was good to see them again after all that time. *so* *you know*
3 It was a shock. I had no idea what they'd been planning. *complete* *at all*
4 It took us an age to get to the top, but it was worth it. The views were stunning. *absolute* *well* *absolutely*
5 The day was amazing. It was better than I'd dared imagine. *whole* *from start to finish* *even*
6 It was the best moment of my life. *without doubt* *single* *entire*

4 **07** Listen and check your ideas for Ex 3. Notice how the voice adds emphasis and enthusiasm.

5 Could any of the sentences in Ex 2 and 3 describe any moments or days in your life? Tell your partner.

Example: *One time we just didn't want the day to end was the other month when …*

6 You are going to tell a partner about one of the best days in your life. Think about these questions and spend a few minutes preparing what you are going to say. Be as emphatic as you can.

When was it?
Where were you?
Who was with you?
What events led up to this day?
How did the day start?
Did you know what was going to happen?
What happened to make it such a good day?
How did you feel at different parts of the day?
What was the single most important moment?
Do you have any special mementos of that day?

Changing the world

Reading

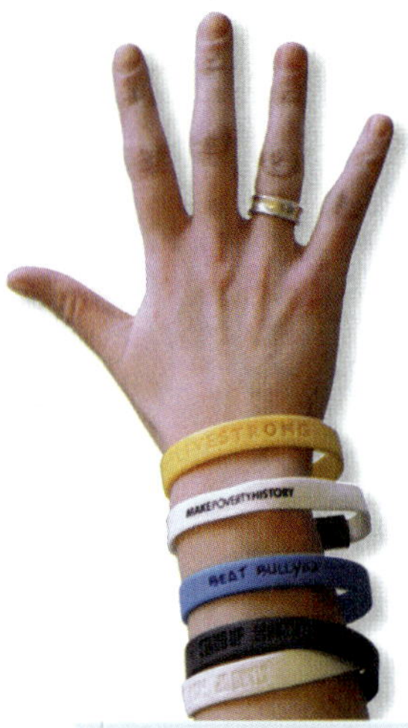

1 Look at the photo. Which of these issues can you see on the wristbands?

cancer	anti-bullying	help for poor countries	racism in football

2 Are you wearing or have you worn a wristband? Are wristbands still a popular way to show public support for campaigns?

3 **08** Read the message board comments. Are these statements true or false? Correct the false ones.

1. According to Jack, wristbands show you belong to a community.
2. Jack thinks it's important to know what message a wristband carries.
3. In Alina's opinion wristbands are just fashion accessories.
4. Fernando thinks supporting a cause is the most important thing.
5. Camille wants people to use more indirect methods of protest and support.
6. Camille thinks people often use donations to charities and campaigns to make them feel good about themselves.

Search

Home Search Shop Bookmarks

On the bandwagon

Do you support important causes by wearing wristbands? Do you think they're an effective way of raising awareness about important issues? Or do you think most people just wear wristbands as a fashion accessory and don't care too much about what they stand for?

I think wristbands are a great way to support a cause. They raise money and they also raise awareness of what that cause is all about. It's like meeting an old friend when you see somebody with the same wristband because you know it means they share the same values as you. But even if other people don't know what a particular wristband represents, it can be a great conversation starter.

Jack, UK

Most people wear wristbands just because they're trendy. They probably don't really care much about the cause, they're just following the crowd. But that still raises awareness of the issue, so if wristbands help spread the word about something, maybe it doesn't matter if they're basically a fashion accessory.

Alina, Romania

I wear a white wristband to express solidarity with a campaign that wants to eradicate poverty. Actually, I don't like wearing things on my wrist but I'm making an exception for this as I think the issue is just so important. Generally, I think it's essential to show commitment to a cause and not just jump on any old bandwagon because it happens to be fashionable.

Fernando, Mexico

Some people use wristbands to say 'Hey look, I've given money to charity, I'm a good person.' Instead of feeling smug because they've done nothing but donate a small amount of money, they should get out on the streets and protest properly for change. That's what we do in France when we want to do something about something. Armchair protests like wristbands, text message campaigns and online petitions don't get you anywhere at all. They just ease your guilty conscience.

Camille, France

4 What do you think? Whose comments do you most agree or disagree with? Why?

Example:
I strongly disagree with Camille's comments. Advances in technology and the importance of global issues mean that newer forms of protest like online petitions are more effective because more people all over the world can participate in them.

5 In your country is it usual to actively support change or raise awareness by protesting in some way? How? What role do mobile phones and the Internet play?

Example:
I come from a country where the government controls the media. The Internet is important because it is an independent source of information. Organising protests by SMS has also become very popular.

Vocabulary and speaking

1 Match the verbs and the nouns. Then check your answers in the text on page 12.

do	express	eradicate
give	raise	raise
show	spread	support

a cause	awareness	commitment	money
money to charity	poverty	solidarity	
something about something	the word		

2 Work in groups and discuss these questions.

Have you ever …
… raised money for a cause? How?
… given money to charity? Which charity? Why?
… spread the word about a cause? How?

Do you currently actively support any causes? Which ones and why?

3 Replace the underlined words with words or phrases from the message board on page 12.

1 Inequality and forms of oppression are topics most people feel strongly about.
2 I've no idea what the letters in UNICEF represent.
3 A current political topic is always a good way of getting a discussion going.
4 It's easier to do what the majority do than swim against the tide.
5 It's unfair to call people self-satisfied just because they try to help.
6 I often have a bad feeling about the fact that we have such easy lives compared to many people in the world.

4 Work with a partner. You are going to discuss an issue using the vocabulary from Ex 1 and Ex 3. Student A, look at page 29. Student B, look at page 32.

Writing

1 Look at the message board discussion topics in the box. Which one do you find most interesting?

animal testing	censorship and state control	computer games and violence	
fair trade	gun control	illegal music downloads	private healthcare
sex discrimination			

2 Think of other possible message board topics with the class.

3 Work in groups. You are going to start your own message boards and write comments on them. Choose a topic and write a brief 'thread' or starting comment (two or three sentences – as in the one in the reading text) on a piece of paper. Make it as interesting and / or controversial as possible and end it with a question.

4 Pass your thread to the person in the group on your right. Respond to the thread you have been given by writing a paragraph. Make sure you put your opinion across clearly.

5 When the 'message boards' have been round the whole group, stop the activity. Read the comments on your board and sum up the general attitude and reactions to your starting comment for the group.

CD-ROM For more activities go to **Individuals Unit 3**

4 No pain, no gain

LEARNING AIMS

- Can talk about success
- Can discuss motivation and overcoming problems
- Can explain causes and results

Getting to the top

Lead-in

1 Work with a partner. Look at these proverbs. Do you have similar proverbs in your language?

a Rome wasn't built in a day.
b Where there's a will, there's a way.
c All work and no play makes Jack a dull boy.
d Look before you leap.
e There's no time like the present.

2 Which of the proverbs in Ex 1 best sums up your attitude to life?

Reading and speaking

1 Work with a partner and discuss these questions.

- What do you know about sumo wrestling? Do you ever watch it?
- What do you think of the sport? What problems might be associated with it?
- What do you think is essential for sumo wrestlers to become champions?

2 09 Read the article on page 15. What problem did Mainoumi have to overcome in order to become a sumo champion? How did he manage it?

3 Which of these things does the article mention? Tick them. Then check your answers in the text and note the adjectives used to describe them.

Mainoumi's speed ☐ his build ☐ his weight ☐ his diet ☐
his family ☐ his command of conventional techniques ☐
his tricks and manoeuvres ☐ his friend ☐ his training ☐ his injuries ☐

4 What other words would you use to describe Mainoumi? What do you think of his actions and achievements?

Vocabulary and speaking

1 Explain the meaning of these idioms from the text.

1 make it big (paragraph 2)
2 by hook or by crook (paragraph 2)

2 Match the idioms to the correct meanings.

1 They got off to a flying start.
2 She won hands down.
3 I passed with flying colours.
4 I was fighting a losing battle.
5 I sailed through it.
6 They stole the show.
7 He decided to throw in the towel.
8 It was a case of sink or swim.

a attracted the most attention
b stopped trying to do something
c began something very well
d being left on one's own to succeed or fail
e trying to do something that would probably fail
f dealt with something very easily
g achieved something with great success
h won very easily

3 Work with a partner. Think about situations involving yourself or people you know which match the idioms in Ex 2. Tell your partner about these situations.

Example:
My driving test got off to a flying start. My parking was excellent and I did a great emergency stop. Unfortunately it was downhill from then on. I saw a car too late at a roundabout and nearly hit it. And then I scraped my wing-mirror on a parked car. I failed the test.

4 In the article, Mainoumi's sumo bouts were described as 'must-see events'. What does *must-see* mean?

5 Work in groups and discuss these questions.

Over the last few years, what have been …

1 the must-see films and TV programmes?
2 the must-see events (sports competitions, matches, concerts, etc)?
3 the must-have gadgets and accessories?
4 the must-have CDs, in your opinion?

A head start for Mainoumi?

'Where there's a will there's a way' is an extremely trite phrase, but in this case, it's hard to think of a more succinct summary. Mainoumi was one of the smallest sumo wrestlers ever, weighing in at 98 kg and 169 cm, only reaching the 173 cm required to wrestle by having an extremely painful silicone implant embedded under his scalp. He was also one of the most exciting wrestlers ever, making up for his pint-sized build with a dizzying array of tricks and manoeuvres that made his bouts the must-see events of his era.

Born Nagao Shuhei in 1967, Mainoumi was a talented sumo wrestler at Nihon University, but knew he could never join the pro ranks because he was too short. Instead, he decided to become a high school teacher, and channelled his love of sumo into mentoring a close friend to become a sumo champion. His friend showed much promise, but during their senior year, the friend died suddenly of an illness. Nagao was heartbroken, and gave up sumo entirely for a few months. But after some reflection, he decided that the best way to honour his friend's memory was to make it big in pro sumo himself, by hook or by crook.

And that is what he did, eventually rising to become the fifth-ranked wrestler in all of sumo. The first challenge was to come up with a way to increase his height from 169 cm to the required 173 cm. After making several inquiries, he finally found a doctor who agreed to implant a sack under his scalp and gradually inject silicone into it over a period of several months. The stretching of his scalp to increase his height by four centimetres meant that Mainoumi had to put up with incredible discomfort, such that he would sometimes throw up or pass out from the pain during his everyday activities. But nevertheless he wrestled throughout his career with the implant, which altogether required four different operations to maintain.

In the ring Mainoumi was nothing short of a sensation. To compensate for his small size, the quick-thinking Mainoumi used dazzling speed, supreme command of conventional techniques, and a willingness to try anything and everything to achieve victory when conventional techniques failed. Perhaps most impressive of all was that Mainoumi was wrestling some of the most massive sumo wrestlers ever. Mainoumi became the ultimate underdog, and a hero to sumo fans everywhere, standing up for the supremacy of wits and technique over size and brute force. Some of the most memorable sumo bouts of the 1990s involved the puny 98 kg Mainoumi facing off against 239 kg Akebono or 275 kg Konishiki.

One of these fights, memorable for all the wrong reasons, was a bout in 1996 when, in a match which Mainoumi actually won, all 275 kilograms of Konishiki came crashing down on Mainoumi's knee, shredding it completely. It took Mainoumi more than a year and a half to make his way back to the ring. He finally made it back in 1999 before a new spate of terrible injuries forced him to retire once and for all at age 32.

Sumo wrestlers must agree to follow the strict rules of their sport.

LANGUAGE STUDY

Three-part phrasal verbs

1 Look at these sentences. Underline the three-part phrasal verbs and match each one with its meaning a–d. The first one has been done for you.

1 *Mainoumi **made up for** his pint-sized build with a dizzying array of tricks and manoeuvres.*
2 *The first challenge was to come up with a way to increase his height from 169 cm to the required 173 cm.*
3 *He had to put up with incredible discomfort.*
4 *Mainoumi stood up for the supremacy of wits and technique over size and brute force.*

a tolerate ☐ b compensate for [1] c defend ☐ d think of ☐

2 All three-part phrasal verbs must have an object. In which position do you always put the object?

Grammar reference page 27

3 Match the beginnings and endings of these quotes. Check your answers on page 32.

1 Too many people **run out of** ideas
2 If your children **look up to** you,
3 I take a simple view of life:
4 The way I see it, if you want the rainbow,
5 It takes a great deal of courage to **stand up to** your enemies,
6 You need to feel good about yourself. The motivation has to come from within.

a but even more to **stand up to** your friends. JK Rowling, author
b You have nobody to **fall back on** except yourself. Dana Hill, actress
c you gotta **put up with** the rain. Dolly Parton, singer
d long before they **run out of** words. Anonymous
e you've made a success of life's biggest job. Anonymous
f keep your eyes open and **get on with** it. Sir Laurence Olivier, actor

4 What is the meaning of the phrasal verbs in **bold** in Ex 3?

5 Which quotation in Ex 3 do you like the best? Compare your ideas with a partner.

6 Complete the extracts with an appropriate form of the phrasal verbs in the box.

come back from	~~come up against~~	come up with	drop out of
face up to	put up with	stand up to	

1 In the 2005 European Cup final, Liverpool *came up against* a rampaging AC Milan. Liverpool __________ being 3–0 down to win on penalties.
2 After being diagnosed with cancer in 1996, world champion cyclist Lance Armstrong had to __________ the possibility that he would never compete again. He went on to win the *Tour de France* a record seven consecutive times.
3 Bill Gates first __________ the idea of setting up a software company while he was a student at Harvard. Against all advice he __________ university to set up the Microsoft Corporation. He was a billionaire by the time he was 30.
4 On 1st December 1955, after __________ years of racial abuse and segregation, Rosa Parks __________ the driver of the bus she was travelling on and refused to give up her seat for a white passenger. She became known as the 'Mother of the modern-day civil rights movement.'

7 Think of someone you know or a famous person who has had to overcome the odds to succeed. Tell your partner.

What motivates you?

Listening

1 10 Listen to four young people talking about their motivation to succeed. Choose the reason for each person's motivation.

a famous person	a friend	an inspirational book	an inspirational family member
a person in history	competition	failure	praise

1 Max ______________ 3 Tom ______________
2 Chloe ______________ 4 Ellen ______________

2 Listen again and answer the questions.

1 What are the positive and negative results of the way Max was brought up?
2 Why was Chloe feeling down?
3 How was Chloe motivated after she watched TV?
4 Why were Tom's parents initially disappointed in him?
5 What was the reaction of Tom's parents to his choice of career?
6 How did Ellen's mother react to getting divorced?

Vocabulary

1 Listen again and complete these sentences. Then check your answers in the listening script on page 31.

1 I think my motivation ______________ my childhood.
2 My confidence today is definitely ______________ the way I was brought up.
3 It's all ______________ Kylie!
4 I love what I'm doing – and that ______________ to try and be better.
5 All my life I've had a very strong ______________.
6 I ______________ everything to my mum.

2 Work in small groups. Talk about what motivates you. Think about these things.

1 Is the source of your motivation something recent or something deeply rooted?
2 Is your motivation the result of a particular experience? Was it positive or negative?
3 Is a particular person responsible for inspiring or motivating you?

Speaking and writing

1 Find the meaning of these words in a dictionary.

cherished genocide huddle machete rip slaughter spree

2 Read the summary of an autobiography. Do you think the book would be inspiring? Why? / Why not? Discuss your ideas with a partner.

3 Choose an inspiring person. Find out information about them and write a blurb of about 120 words for the back cover of a biography of their life.

Left to tell by Imaculee Ilibagiza

Immaculee Ilibagiza grew up in a country she loved, surrounded by a family she cherished. But in 1994 her idyllic world was ripped apart as Rwanda descended into bloody genocide. Immaculee's family was brutally murdered during a killing spree that lasted three months and claimed the lives of nearly a million Rwandans. Incredibly, Immaculee survived the slaughter. For 91 days, she and seven other women huddled silently together in the cramped bathroom of a local pastor, while hundreds of machete-wielding killers hunted for them. The triumphant story of this remarkable young woman's journey through the darkness of genocide will inspire anyone whose life has been touched by fear, suffering, and loss.

CD-ROM For more activities go to **Individuals Unit 4**

5 Review

Lead-in 1 Are there any websites that you visit regularly or that you really like? Which websites do you have bookmarked in your 'favourites'?

Million dollar boy

1 Look at the photo of the Million Dollar homepage. Can you guess what it consists of?

2 11 Listen to the news story and check your ideas in Ex 1.

3 What do the figures represent? Listen again and check.

Example: 100,000 – *He made £100,000 during the first week at university.*

1 a million ☐ 2 2005 ☐ 3 100 ☐ 4 6,400 ☐ 5 21 ☐
6 40,000 and 60,000 ☐ 7 1000 and 38 ☐ 8 tens of thousands ☐

4 Complete these extracts with an appropriate form of the three-part phrasal verbs in the box.

be down to	come up with	drop out of	fall back on	get on with	run out of

1 While most of his fellow students were already ______________ what little cash they had during fresher's week, Nottingham University student Alex Tew made over £100,000.
2 Alex Tew ______________ the idea one night in August 2005.
3 The fees and accommodation for the first year alone were starting to look daunting, and with no finances to ______________ Alex was dreading running up huge debts.
4 Alex immediately ______________ setting up the website.
5 And not for one minute did Alex consider ______________ university.
6 Experts agree that the Million Dollar Homepage's success ______________ three things: the power of word of mouth, that it's the rags-to-riches story of an ordinary student and that it was a truly innovative yet simple idea.

5 Look at this summary of the story of the Million Dollar Homepage. Complete the descriptions of the nouns in **bold** by adding the words and phrases in *italics* in an appropriate order.

Example:
Alex Tew was accepted on a **course**. *degree* *which started in September 2005* *at Nottingham University* *business management*

Alex Tew was accepted on a business management degree course at Nottingham University, which started in September 2005.

1 He was worried about his **situation** and the **debts**. *that he would be running up* *huge* *financial*
2 He came up with the **idea** of a **website**. *that he would sell to advertisers for a dollar a pixel* *made up of a million pixels* *consisting of just one page* *ingenious*
3 Alex decided the web page would need a **name**. He thought of and bought the **name** 'milliondollarhomepage.com' that **evening**. *same* *memorable* *domain* *that would capture the imagination*
4 Most of the **companies** reported an **increase** in the number of **hits** as well as **sales**. *increased* *immediate* *that bought webspace* *on their websites*
5 **Websites** copied Alex's idea, but none achieved anything like the **success**. *of the Million Dollar Homepage* *numerous other* *phenomenal*

Does Alex Tew deserve his million dollars?

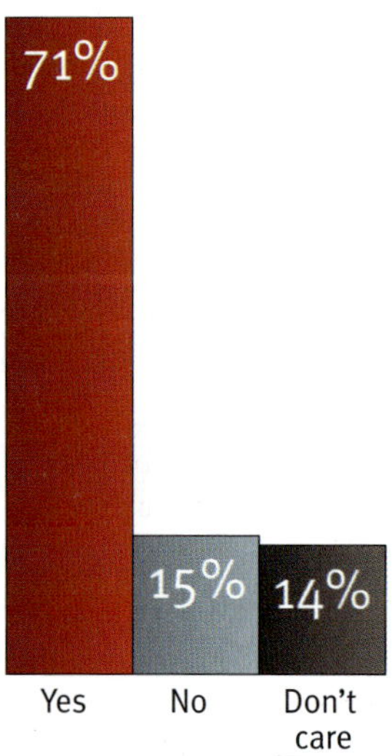

6 The chart shows the results of an internet survey. What is your opinion and why?

Innovation

1 Choose the correct alternative in these extracts from an article called 'Beds in the boardroom'.

1. We tend to associate lying down with being tired and emptying the mind, *on the other hand / nevertheless / yet* research has shown that we think more clearly and innovatively when lying down.
2. When we are standing, the brain produces more of the chemical noradrenalin, which slows brain activity. When we are lying down, *however / while / yet*, production of noradrenalin is reduced and thinking speeds can increase by 10%.
3. *But / However / While* meetings are where ideas are supposed to be generated, about 80% of us have our best work-related ideas outside the workplace and one in five of us when we're lying in bed.
4. *Even though / On the other hand / Yet* there is evidence supporting the idea of making meetings more informal and relaxed, we are still a long way from beds in the boardroom.
5. Business managers believe that sitting upright makes people get to the point quicker, *yet / whereas / on the other hand* they fear that a more relaxed atmosphere could make meetings drag on.

2 Where do you do your best thinking and have your best ideas?

3 Are you an innovator or more suited to turning other people's ideas into a success? Complete the questionnaire.

How innovative are you?

Choose the circle that is closest to the word that best describes you.

1	My outlook on life is generally:	realistic	○ ○ ○ ○	optimistic
2	A word that describes me most of the time is:	serious	○ ○ ○ ○	frivolous
3	A word that describes me most of the time is:	conventional	○ ○ ○ ○	unorthodox
4	I am more concerned with:	issues at home and work	○ ○ ○ ○	causes outside work
5	I tend to be more:	process-orientated	○ ○ ○ ○	people-orientated
6	A word that describes me most of the time is:	accepting	○ ○ ○ ○	curious
7	A word that describes me most of the time is:	logical	○ ○ ○ ○	visionary
8	I know the eye colour of my ten closest friends.	none of them	○ ○ ○ ○	all of them

4 Add up your score from the questionnaire (from left to right score 1, 2, 3, 4) and read the analysis.

Your final score: 25–32
You're a **right-brain** thinker, meaning you tend to draw on your emotional, creative side the most. You are curious, with a vivid imagination and you have innovative ideas. But you need to be partnered by a left-brainer who can help you bring your ideas to fruition.

Your final score: 17–24
You're a **whole-brain** thinker, meaning you have easy access to both sides of your brain. This allows you to come up with great new ideas and put them into action. Whole-brainers tend to be natural innovators and entrepreneurs who can often go it alone.

Your final score: 8–16
You're a **left-brain** thinker. Left-brainers are logical, analytical, and organised, and are well suited for turning a good idea into a reality. Your ideal partner is a right-brain visionary who will help you look at situations creatively and provide you with initial ideas.

5 Discuss these questions with a partner.

1. Are you a right-, left- or whole-brain thinker? Is the analysis of you accurate?
2. Do you think Alex Tew is a right-, left- or whole-brain thinker?
3. Which famous people do you think are right-, left- and whole-brain thinkers?

It is without doubt the single most important invention of all time.

It's so important. Without it, life just wouldn't be the same at all.

It was absolutely pivotal.

It is by far the greatest innovation ever.

Speaking

1 A recent survey asked people to vote for the greatest 'everyday' innovation in each of the following categories. Work in groups and discuss what you think the winners should be.

Communications	Household	The arts and music	Transport

2 Turn to page 29 to see which innovation won each category.

3 You are going to give a brief presentation. Follow these instructions.

- Work in groups of four. Each person selects a different innovation from the category winners on page 29.
- Prepare a two-minute presentation explaining why your innovation should win. Be as emphatic as you can. Use the ideas in the speech bubbles and the Language study on page 11 to help you.
- Take turns to give your presentations.
- When you have all spoken, vote for the winner. You can't vote for your innovation.

4 Look at page 32 to see which innovation was the overall winner in the survey.

Vocabulary

1 Read how to play 'Win hands down' and then play the game.

Win hands down

How to play

1 Play in two teams of two or three players each.
2 Team A chooses a sentence for team B. If team B thinks the sentence is correct they 'keep it' and if they think it is incorrect they 'give it' to team A. Cross off this sentence so it cannot be used again.
3 Team B then chooses a sentence for team A and so on. Keep a record of which team has which sentences.
4 When all the sentences have been used, check the answers on page 32. You get one point for each correct sentence you have. The team with the highest score wins.

1 They got off to a flying start.	**2** She's a bit of loser.	**3** I really look up at her.	**4** It's quite cheap-looking.	**5** They came up against a lot of opposition.	**6** He's rather inorthodox.
7 It's driving me mad.	**8** It was must-watching TV.	**9** It was a non-violent protest.	**10** She's got an avid imagination.	**11** She's very softly-spoken.	**12** They are fighting a lose battle.
13 It's very bright-coloured.	**14** He followed in his father's footprints.	**15** I'm fed up with it.	**16** It's a time-saving device.	**17** It's bad-made.	**18** He did a lot to raise the word.
19 They stole the show.	**20** It's got an oval-shape window.	**21** They ran out with good ideas.	**22** I think they'll make it big.	**23** It's not very children-friendly.	**24** He should throw in the towel.
25 He did a lot for civilian rights.	**26** It's just a fashion accessory.	**27** She supports a lot of causes.	**28** He's an obsessing collector.	**29** It's the current must-have CD.	**30** I passed with flying colour.

2 Can you think of someone or something that can be described by each of the sentences in the game? Share your ideas.

Song

1 Read the factfile about KT Tunstall and answer these questions.
1 What is her musical background?
2 What prejudice did she face getting a record deal?
3 What was the turning point in her career?

factfile

KT Tunstall was born in 1975 to a Chinese mother and Irish father, but was adopted as a baby by a Scottish couple and raised in St Andrews in Scotland. She was musical from an early age, learning to play piano, flute and guitar as a teenager.

KT spent some time studying in the USA and then returned to the UK to do a music course at Royal Holloway College in London, before moving back to St Andrews. She became involved in the local music scene, where she served her musical apprenticeship before moving back to London to start her solo career. Her attempts to get a record deal were thwarted by constantly being told that at 25 she was too old to start a successful career as a recording artist. KT's big break came when she appeared on a TV show as a last-minute replacement for another act. She brought the house down and was suddenly in great demand. Her first album *Eye to the telescope*, which includes the song *Suddenly I see*, was released in 2004 to great critical acclaim.

2 **12** Listen to the song *Suddenly I see* and read the lyrics.
1 What does she 'suddenly see'?
2 Who do you think she is singing about?

3 Look at the picture and read the quote on page 29 to check your answers to Ex 2.

4 Listen to the song again. How do you interpret these lyrics?
1 Her face is a map of the world
2 I feel like walking the world
3 She likes to leave you hanging on a word
4 She makes me feel like I could be a tower

5 Are you, or were you, inspired in any way by someone famous? Tell a partner.

Suddenly I see

Her face is a map of the world, is a map of the world
You can see she's a beautiful girl, she's a beautiful girl
And everything around her is a silver pool of light
People who surround her feel the benefit of it
It makes you calm
She holds you captivated in her palm

Chorus

Suddenly I see
This is what I wanna be
Suddenly I see
Why the hell it means so much to me

And I feel like walking the world, like walking the world
And you can hear she's a beautiful girl, she's a beautiful girl
She fills up every corner like she's born in black and white
Makes you feel warmer when you're trying to remember
What you heard
She likes to leave you hanging on a word

Chorus

And she's taller than most and she's looking at me
I can see her eyes looking from the page in a magazine
She makes me feel like I could be a tower, big strong tower, yeah
The power to be, the power to give, the power to see, yeah yeah

Suddenly I see
She got the power to be
The power to give
The power to see yeah yeah

Chorus

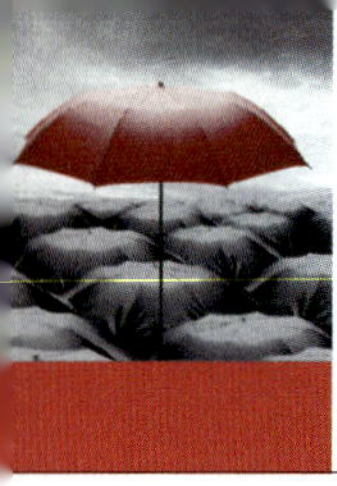

Extra practice

Unit 1

1 Complete the puzzle with the character and behaviour adjectives. Do you agree with the advice in the shaded column?

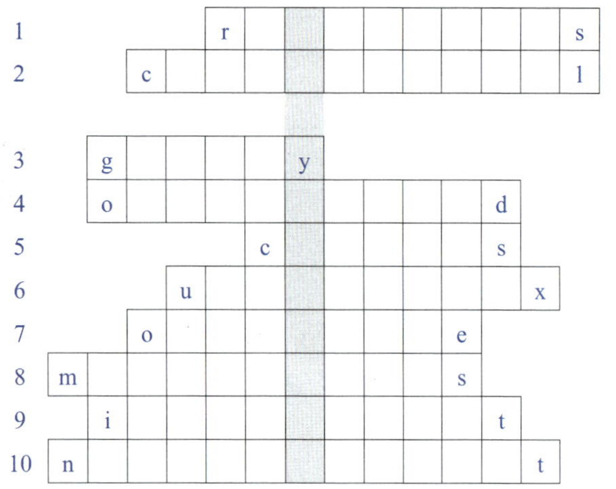

1 opposing authority or the accepted rules of society.
2 following the usual and accepted opinions and ways of behaving, especially without questioning them.
3 feeling sad and without hope.
4 having very strong opinions and refusing to change them even when they are clearly unreasonable.
5 wanting to find out about things.
6 not following the usual rules or beliefs of your religion, society, etc.
7 always thinking about someone or something that is important to you, in a way that seems extreme to other people.
8 enjoying having fun by causing trouble, used especially to describe a child.
9 good at thinking clearly and quickly, at understanding difficult ideas and subjects, and at gaining and using knowledge.
10 different from the way most people usually think or behave.

2 Which noun from the box collocates with each set of adjectives?

collector imagination outlook side traits

1 positive / gloomy / sunny ____________
2 avid / keen / obsessive ____________
3 unusual / unorthodox / eccentric ____________
4 dark / funny / creative ____________
5 fertile / overactive / vivid ____________

3 Read the article and complete it by putting an appropriate contrastive discourse marker in each space. Choose from those in the box and use each at least once.

even though however nevertheless whereas / while yet

Japanese inventor Dr NakaMats has been officially recognised as one of the five most influential scientists in history, (1) __________ his accomplishments are all-too-often overlooked and people tend to focus instead on his unique lifestyle and somewhat eccentric personality.

Dr NakaMats holds the all-time record for patents with over 3,200 inventions to date, surpassing the great inventor Thomas Edison. And (2) __________ many of Edison's patents were for already existing inventions to which Edison simply put his name, Dr NakaMats' patents are all his own work. His inventions include the digital watch, the floppy disk and the less notable and yet-to-catch-on 'Bouncing Shoes'.

According to Dr NakaMats, in order to be a great inventor, you must be born with special abilities. He believes that (3)__________ engineers and researchers generally find their solutions through trial and error, the inventor will, at some point during the invention process, experience a flash of revelation. 'If a team of engineers works hard enough and long enough, they will eventually be able to make small improvements in technology. (4) __________, only true inventors are able to devise breakthroughs that change the world overnight,' Dr NakaMats explains. He firmly believes that (5) __________ engineering can be learned, inventing is an innate ability that people are born with.

(6) __________ most people of Dr NakaMats' age (he was born in 1928) are enjoying their twilight years, he works out lifting weights on a daily basis, stays away from doctors and conventional medicine and confidently predicts he will live to 144. And (7) __________ he eats only one meal a day (of 700 calories) and sleeps exactly four hours a night (from 4am to 8am) he is (8) __________ in perfect health.

Unit 2

1 Rewrite these newspaper extracts to include one or more compound adjectives so that the meaning is the same.

Example:
The main course was followed by a selection of fruit that made the mouth water.

The main course was followed by a selection of mouth-watering fruit.

1 **The family escaped the blaze by jumping out of a window on the second floor.**

The family escaped the blaze by jumping out of ______________________________.

2 **All their products are made by hand.**

All their products ______________________________.

3 **She was wearing a black and gold dress that caught the eye.**

She was wearing ______________________________
______________________________.

4 **It is one of the records in sport that has stood for the longest.**

It is one of ______________________________
______________________________.

2 Make compound adjectives.

1	well- / badly	a	coloured
2	good- / expensive-	b	known
3	well- / little-	c	day
4	smartly / casually	d	paid
5	heart- / diamond-	e	shaped
6	broad- / open-	f	looking
7	environment- / child-	g	spoken
8	well- / softly	h	based
9	multi- / brightly	i	minded
10	European- / Tokyo-	j	friendly
11	energy- / time-	k	dressed
12	all- / modern-	l	saving

3 Write six more compound adjectives that include some of the words in Ex 2.

Example: *poorly paid, strange-looking*

4 Look at the example and write similar one-sentence descriptions of the famous people, places and things.

Example:
He's a businessman. He's American. He was born in 1955. He dropped out of Harvard University. He went on to become a billionaire before he was 30.

He's an American businessman born in 1955, who dropped out of Harvard University, and who went on to become a billionaire before he was 30.

1 It's a device. It's hand-held. It allows you to talk to other people wherever you are.

____
____

2 It's a mode of transport. It's two-wheeled. It was invented by a Scotsman in the mid-1800s.

____
____

3 It's a statue. It's of a human figure. It's got outstretched arms. It overlooks Rio de Janeiro in Brazil.

____
____

4 He's an actor. He's American. He was born in 1963. He is of British, German and Cherokee Indian descent.

____
____

5 Which people, places and things are described in Ex 4? Check your answers at the bottom of the page.

6 Complete the mini-dialogues with the words in the box.

alone bad fed up mad moaning poor problems sick sock

1 A: I'm totally __________ of this dreadful weather.
B: Oh, stop __________ about it! Anyway, it's going to be nicer tomorrow.

2 A: I can't even afford new socks let __________ a new pair of shoes.
B: Come on, it can't be that __________.

3 A: I've had this awful cold for days now. I just can't get anything done. It's driving me __________.
B: Oh, __________ you! Are you taking anything for it?

4 A: I'm totally __________ with absolutely everything at the moment. If it's not one thing, it's another.
B: Oh, put a __________ in it. You're not the only one with __________, you know.

7 Complete these sentences so they are true for you.

1 I'm sick and tired of ______________________________.

2 I'm fed up with ______________________________.

3 ______________________________ drives me mad.

Example: Bill Gates 1 mobile phone 2 bicycle
3 statue of Christ the Redeemer 4 Johnny Depp

Unit 3

1 Complete the newspaper headlines with the words and phrases in the box. The country and date in brackets will help you.

apartheid	civil rights movement	democratic rule	equality	military rulers	non-violent protest	segregation

1 Civil Rights Act outlaws all racial __________. (USA, 1964)

2 Four students killed as national guardsmen open fire on __________ (Ohio, USA, 1970)

3 __________ restored after 17 years as __________ stand down (Chile, 1990)

4 __________ for all as __________ officially ended (South Africa, 1994)

5 'Mother of the modern __________' Rosa Parks dies. (USA, 2005)

2 Rewrite these sentences putting the words in *italics* in an appropriate position to add emphasis.

1 They are the greatest band. *by far ever*

____

2 It was a mistake. It looks worse than before. *huge even*

____

3 There's no chance of it happening in the near future. *absolutely at all*

____

4 They are cheaper than when they came out. *loads first*

____

5 I don't understand what they were thinking of. It's ugly. *just so*

____

6 The thing was a disaster. *whole total from start to finish*

____

3 Think of something or someone that each of the sentences in Ex 2 could be describing.

1 *Sugababes*　　4 __________
2 __________　　5 __________
3 __________　　6 __________

4 Complete the website forum using the words and phrases in the boxes.

by far	single	vast

Buffet $37 billion giveaway

The second richest man in the world, investor Warren Buffet, has announced that he is going to donate the (1) _____ majority of his wealth, namely $37 billion, to charity. Buffet's donation is (2) _____ the (3) _____ biggest philanthropic act in history. Click here to have your say on this great giveaway.

anywhere	awesome	simply

I applaud Mr Buffet for his (4) _____ generosity, but everyone knows that the vast proportion of money donated 'disappears' and (5) _____ doesn't get to the people who actually need it. After Live Aid 80% of the money didn't get (6) _____ near those who needed it.

Russ, Sheffield, UK

at all	highly	just	much	real	very

While the money Mr Buffet has given away is indeed (7)_____ commendable, I think it's a (8)_____ shame that it took him so long to do so. After all, he's been a multi-billionaire for a (9)_____ long time now. Also, I remember Mr Buffet once saying that he believed that educating a person goes (10)_____ farther than giving away cash. So, why is he doing the opposite? I (11)_____ don't understand it (12)_____.

Jakob, Berlin

5 Complete the sentences with the verbs in the box.

eradicate	express	raise	show	spread

1 The demonstration was to __________ solidarity with the sacked workers and to inform the board and shareholders alike that the dismissals will not be taken lying down.
2 With 15% of the world's population going hungry every day, the need to __________ poverty is as great today as it has ever been.
3 The campaign is designed to __________ awareness among primary-aged schoolchildren of the need to eat sensibly.
4 To __________ support for the worldwide 'kindness' day, people are being asked to wear something with a heart on it.
5 Environmentalists were distributing 'If you care, car share' car stickers to __________ the word about the campaign to cut congestion.

Unit 4

1 Match the two halves of these proverbs.

1	Where there's a will,	a	like the present
2	All work and no play	b	in a day
3	Rome wasn't built	c	leap
4	Look before you	d	there's a way
5	There's no time	e	makes Jack a dull boy

2 Complete these sports headlines with the idioms in the box.

flying colours   flying start   hands down
sail through   sink or swim   steals the show

1 Woods off to a ______________ with six birdies and an eagle in first round of US open

2 Tampa Bay Buccaneers ______________ to next round with 75-6 win

3 Jian ______________ at World Championships with perfect 10 for floor routine

4 Palmer wins ______________, 6-1, 6-0

5 All Blacks pass first test match with ______________.

6 It's ______________ for 'The Mariners' as League One relegation battle looms

3 Complete these newspaper extracts with an appropriate form of the three-part phrasal verbs in the box.

come back from   come up against
face up to   ~~get on with~~   look up to
make up for   put up with   run out of

1 'We've just got to (1) *get on with it* and go out on Saturday and win the game. Our destiny is in our own hands,' says goalkeeper Tom MacAlister. 'Last season we (2) __________ being five points adrift at the foot of the table with only three games to go and managed to avoid relegation. I'm confident we can do so again.'

2 Tiger's opening round of 63 and 6-stroke first-day lead will go a long way in (3) __________ his disappointment at finishing in tenth place in last year's event.

3 The American absolutely dominated the match, which lasted a mere 36 minutes. It seemed that opponent Kuchova simply (4) __________ energy and motivation mid-way through the second set, in which she didn't win a single game.

4 The British Lions (5) __________ a rampaging New Zealand in Christchurch yesterday and could do little but watch as the All Blacks ran in nine tries. 'We need to (6) __________ the reality that we were simply second-best in the game and we have a long way to go,' said coach Andrew Robinson.

5 The Miami Dolphins had to (7) __________ driving rain as well as a rampant Tampa Bay as they were well and truly beaten by 11 touchdowns to one.

6 'We've always (8) __________ Russia and other Eastern European nations, and we still do, but now we are competing with them as equals.' said the gold-medal winning Chinese gymnast.

4 Match the sports with the headlines in Ex 2 and the extracts in Ex 3.

	Sport	Headline	Extract
1	football	*6*	*1*
2	American football		
3	golf		
4	gymnastics		
5	rugby		
6	tennis		

5 Complete these extracts with an expression using *must-* and the words in the box.

have (x2)   see   visit   watch   win

1 For its first few series after it was first broadcast in 1999, *Big Brother* was without doubt the ____________ programme of its day.

2 Argentina go into their ____________ match against Germany with a number of injury worries.

3 Every Harry Potter release was the ____________ film of the year for the majority of under-twelves, and many adults alike.

4 Making the Walkman and portable CD player almost redundant overnight, the iPod instantly became the ____________ gadget for any self-respecting teenager and twenty-something.

5 Poll after poll puts *What's going on?* by Marvin Gaye as the number one ____________ album of all time.

6 Whether passing through in a day or on holiday, Central Park, the Empire State Building and Fifth Avenue are the ____________ places when in New York.

Grammar reference

Unit 1

Contrast

The most common contrastive linkers (discourse markers) are:

but

But is the most common contrastive linker in English.

You can use *but* in conjunction with other contrastive linkers. For example, *but nevertheless …, but whereas …*

You use *but* between two contrasting ideas.
It was sunny, ***but*** *a bit cold.*
Jane knows all about the party, ***but*** *please don't tell her you know.*
We were exhausted, ***but nevertheless*** *we continued.*

yet

Yet emphasises that something is surprising.

You use *yet* between the two contrasting ideas in a sentence.

He is colour blind, ***yet*** *his paintings are full of colour.*

however

However is more formal than *but* and can suggest that something is surprising or unexpected.

You use *however* at the beginning of the second sentence, after the subject in the second sentence or at the end of the second sentence.
I'm terrible at remembering names. ***However,*** *I never forget a face.*
He was confident he had the right credentials. His interviewers, ***however,*** *were not impressed.*

on the other hand

On the other hand balances two ideas that contrast but do not contradict. You can use it when you are trying to be fair and moderate.

You use *on the other hand* at the beginning of the second sentence, after the subject in the second sentence or at the end of the second sentence.
She tends to keep herself to herself. Her sister, ***on the other hand,*** *is very outgoing.*

whereas / while

Whereas and *while* balance two ideas that contrast, but do not contradict. The meaning of *whereas* and *while* is basically the same.

You use *whereas* and *while* before the first or second idea in the sentence.
Top players' wages have risen astronomically, ***whereas*** *those in the lower leagues have seen little rise in pay, at all.*
While *it hasn't yet been officially announced, it is believed the president has offered his resignation.*

nevertheless

Nevertheless expresses that something happens when something else makes it seem unlikely. It is quite formal.

You use *nevertheless* at the beginning of the second sentence, after the subject in the second sentence or at the end of the second sentence.
E-commerce is a difficult area to do well in. ***Nevertheless,*** *tens of thousands of new businesses start up every year.*
He was advised against making a formal complaint. He went ahead and did it nevertheless.

even though / although / despite / in spite of

Even though / although / despite / in spite of express that something happens when something else makes it seem unlikely.

You use *even though / although / despite / in spite of* at the beginning of the subordinate clause (the idea that makes the other seem unlikely).
They carried on walking ***even though*** *the rain was pouring down.*
Although *sales aren't what we'd been hoping for, they're quite encouraging.*
Most of the people I spoke to had never seen the film. ***Despite*** *this, everyone seemed familiar with its content.*

Auxiliary *do*

You can use the auxiliary verb *do* to show and emphasise contrast.
It rained all day, but we ***did*** *have a good time.*
I ***do*** *agree, honest.*

Unit 2

Describing buildings, places and objects

You can add descriptive detail to nouns by adding:

- adjectives – including present and past participles used as adjectives, and nouns used as adjectives (defining nouns)
- relative clauses
- clauses beginning with a present or past participle (participle clauses)
- phrases beginning with a preposition.

Adjectives, present and past participles used as adjectives, and nouns used as adjectives come before the noun.
*It was a **lovely** day.*
*The **twisting** road stretched for miles.*
*There are lots of **recently built** apartments.*
*She lost her **wedding** ring.*
*We stayed in a **tiny beach** hut.*

Relative clauses, clauses beginning with a present or past participle and phrases beginning with a preposition come after the noun.
*We went to that restaurant **that your sister recommended**.*
*Is this the book **you were talking about**?*
*The man **standing over there** is the new sales manager.*
*That's the hotel **featured in the paper** the other day.*
*The café **next to the park** has good coffee.*

Unit 3

Adding emphasis

You can add emphasis in many different ways. Some of the more common ways are as follows. Note that you can use some words (*just*, *even*, etc) in more than one way.

You can add emphasis to nouns using certain adjectives:
*I have a **terrible** cold.*
*The **vast** majority disagreed with the proposal.*
*It's an **absolute** disgrace.*
*That's the **single** most disgusting thing I've ever eaten.*
*The **whole** day was brilliant.*
*It was a **total** waste of time.*

You can add emphasis to adjectives using certain adverbs:
*She was **absolutely** delighted.*
*It's **really** great to see you.*
*The film was **just** amazing.*
*It was **even** better than we'd imagined.*
*It's **so** difficult to know what to do.*
*It's **by far** the most amazing place I've been to.*
*He was **all** alone.*

You can add emphasis to verbs or verb clauses using certain adverbs:
*We **just** stood there in amazement.*
*I **really** couldn't believe it.*
*I didn't **even** have time to say hello.*

You can add more general emphasis to what you are saying using certain phrases, which usually occur at the beginning or end of a clause:
*I couldn't hear anything **at all**.*
*It was **without doubt** her best film to date.*
*It was great **from start to finish**.*
*I didn't regret it **for a moment**.*

When speaking you can use the phrase *you know* to add emphasis. This is quite informal, but very common.
*It was unbelievable, **you know**.*
***You know**, I've never seen anything like it.*

Unit 4

Three-part phrasal verbs

Form

Three-part phrasal verbs comprise a verb with two particles.

to put up with
to run out of

Three-part phrasal verbs are transitive and therefore must always take an object. The object always goes after the second particle.
I'll get back to **you** later. (not: ~~*I'll get back you to later*~~ or ~~*I'll get you back to later*~~.)

Use and meaning

The meaning of a three-part phrasal verb is not the same as the independent meaning of the verb and particles. Most three-part phrasal verbs have only one meaning (unlike many two-part phrasal verbs which can have multiple meanings).

Here are some common three-part phrasal verbs (and their meanings).
catch up with (reach the same level or position), *come back from* (to be successful after being in a bad situation), *come back to* (return to), *come down with* (become ill with), *come out with* (say), *come up with* (think of), *cut down on* (reduce), *drop out of* (leave something, such as a course, before you have finished it), *fall back on* (use when other things have failed), *get away with* (avoid discovery), *get back to* (to phone, write or speak to somebody at a later time), *get on with* (do), *get round to* (find time to do), *get up to* (do), *look up to* (respect), *keep up with* (stay at the same level as), *look down on* (think you are better than), *look forward to* (feel excited about something that is going to happen), *make up for* (compensate for), *put up with* (tolerate), *run out of* (have no more of / use all of), *stand up for* (defend), *stand / face up to* (face)

*My printer has **run out of** ink.*
*I need to **catch up with** the work I missed last week.*
*I'm so **looking forward to** the end of term.*
*Is there anything you can **fall back on**?*

Wordlist

*** the 2,500 most common English words, ** very common words, * fairly common words

Unit 1

aberrant *adj* /æ'berənt/
avid *adj* /'ævɪd/
Before you comment, can I just ... *phr* /bɪ'fɔː juː ˌkɒment kən aɪ ˌdʒʌst/
By the way ... *expr* /ˌbaɪ ðə 'weɪ/
Can I add something? *phr* /kən aɪ 'æd ˌsʌmθɪŋ/
Can I finish what I was saying? *phr* /kən aɪ ˌfɪnɪʃ ˌwɒt aɪ wəz 'seɪɪŋ/
collector *n* /kə'lektə/ **
colour blind *adj* /'kʌlə ˌblaɪnd/ **
conformity *n* /kən'fɔːməti/
conventional *adj* /kən'venʃnəl/ ***
creative *adj* /kri'eɪtɪv/ **
curious *adj* /'kjʊəriəs/ **
dark *adj* /dɑːk/ ***
eccentric *adj* /ɪk'sentrɪk/
eccentricity *n* /ˌeksen'trɪsəti/
Er, yeah ... Anyway *expr* /ɜː jeə... 'eniweɪ/
excel (in) *v* /ɪk'sel (ɪn)/
exhaustive *adj* /ɪg'zɔːstɪv/
feminine *adj* /'femənɪn/ *
fertile *adj* /'fɜːtaɪl/ *
gloomy *adj* /'gluːmi/ *
Hang on! *expr* /'hæŋ ˌɒn/
incidence *n* /'ɪnsɪdəns/ *
Incidentally *expr* /ˌɪnsɪ'dentli/ *
individuality *n* /ˌɪndɪˌvɪdʒʊ'æləti/
invasion *n* /ɪn'veɪʒn/ **
Just let me finish, please *phr* /ˌdʒʌst ˌlet miː 'fɪnɪʃ ˌpliːz/
keen *adj* /kiːn/ ***
manifest itself *v* /'mænɪfest ɪtˌself/ *
mischievous *adj* /'mɪstʃɪvəs/
obsessive *adj* /əb'sesɪv/
opinionated *adj* /ə'pɪnjəˌneɪtɪd/
optimistic *adj* /ˌɒptɪ'mɪstɪk/ **
outlook *n* /'aʊtˌlʊk/ *
overactive *adj* /ˌəʊvər'æktɪv/
persona *n* /pə'səʊnə/
positive *adj* /'pɒzətɪv/ ***
privacy *n* /'prɪvəsi/ *
rebellious *adj* /rɪ'beljəs/
retrospective *adj* /ˌretrəʊ'spektɪv/ *
scandalous *adj* /'skændələs/
side *n* /saɪd/ ***
Sorry to interrupt *phr* /ˌsɒri tuː ɪntə'rʌpt/
sympathetic *adj* /ˌsɪmpə'θetɪk/ **
That reminds me ... *phr* /ˌðæt rɪ'maɪndz ˌmiː/
To get back to what I was saying before *phr* /tə ˌget bæk tə ˌwɒt aɪ wəz ˌseɪɪŋ bɪ'fɔː/
trait *n* /treɪt/ *
unconventional *adj* /ˌʌnkən'venʃnəl/
unorthodox *adj* /ʌn'ɔːθəˌdɒks/ *
vivid *adj* /'vɪvɪd/ *
Wait a minute! *phr* /'weɪt ə ˌmɪnɪt/
Where was I? *expr* /ˌweə 'wɒz ˌaɪ/

Unit 2

adhere to *v* /əd'hɪə tuː/
(Zurich)-based *adj* /('zjʊərɪk) ˌbeɪst/
Cheer up! *expr* /ˌtʃɪər 'ʌp/
Come on, it can't be that bad. *expr* /'kʌm ˌɒn ɪt ˌkɑːnt bɪ 'ðæt ˌbæd/
copper *n* /'kɒpə/ **
crumb *n* /krʌm/
desecrate *v* /'desɪˌkreɪt/
desirable *adj* /dɪ'zaɪrəbl/ **
despise *v* /dɪ'spaɪz/
dome *n* /dəʊm/
drive sb mad *expr* /ˌdraɪv ... 'mæd/
(window)-facing *adj* /('wɪndəʊ) ˌfeɪsɪŋ/
fed up with (+ -ing) *expr* /'fed ˌʌp wɪð/
(environment)-friendly *adj* /(ɪn'vaɪrənmənt) ˌfrendli/
functional *adj* /'fʌŋkʃnəl/ **
How awful! *expr* /ˌhaʊ 'ɔːfl/
let alone *expr* /'let əˌləʊn/
(frivolous)-looking *adj* /('frɪvələs) ˌlʊkɪŋ/
(much)-loved *adj* /('mʌtʃ) ˌlʌvd/
make a mental note *expr* /ˌmeɪk ə ˌmentl 'nəʊt/
miss *v* /mɪs/ ***
motif *n* /məʊ'tiːf/ *
multi-coloured *adj* /ˌmʌlti 'kʌləd/
novelty *n* /'nɒvlti/ *
Oh, change the record! *expr* /ˌəʊ 'tʃeɪndʒ ðə ˌrekɔːd/
Oh, dear, I'm sorry. *expr* /ˌəʊ ˌdɪə ˌaɪm 'sɒri/
Oh, just shut up. *expr* /ˌəʊ ˌdʒʌst 'ʃʌt ʌp/
Oh, poor you! *expr* /ˌəʊ 'pʊə juː/
overflowing (with) *adj* /ˌəʊvə'fləʊɪŋ (wɪð)/
peckish *adj* /'pekɪʃ/
penetrate *v* /'penətreɪt/ **
perched *adj* /'pɜːtʃt/
plateau *n* /'plætəʊ/
postwar *adj* /ˌpəʊst'wɔː/ *
Put a sock in it! *expr* /ˌpʊt ə 'sɒk ɪn ɪt/
quaint *adj* /'kweɪnt/
rebuilding *n* /ˌriː'bɪldɪŋ/ **
redbrick *adj* /'redˌbrɪk/
ruined *adj* /'ruːɪnd/ **
rummage *v* /'rʌmɪdʒ/
(energy)-saving *adj* /('enədʒi) ˌseɪvɪŋ/
schedule *v* /'ʃedjuːəl/ **
sensuous *adj* /'sensjuəs/
(pie)-shaped *adj* /('paɪ) ʃeɪpt/
sick of (+ -ing) *expr* /'sɪk əv/
smart *adj* /smɑːt/ **
soothing *adj* /'suːðɪŋ/
sophistication *n* /səˌfɪstɪ'keɪʃn/
sparkling *adj* /'spɑːklɪŋ/
Stop moaning! *expr* /ˌstɒp 'məʊnɪŋ/
(three)-storey *adj* /('θriː) ˌstɔːri/ *
ultra *adv* /'ʌltrə/
universally-acclaimed *adj* /'juːnɪˌvɜːsəli əˌkleɪmd/
well-known *adj* /ˌwel 'nəʊn/ **
well-maintained *adj* /ˌwel meɪn'teɪnd/
What a shame! *expr* /ˌwɒt ə 'ʃeɪm/
workspace *n* /'wɜːkspeɪs/

Unit 3

a single person (at all) *expr* /ə 'sɪŋgl ˌpɜːsn (ət 'ɔːl)/
absolute *adj* /'æbsəluːt/ **
absolutely *adv* /'æbsəluːtli/ ***
anti-bullying *n* /ˌænti 'bʊliɪŋ/
apartheid *n* /ə'pɑːtˌheɪt; ə'pɑːtˌhaɪd/
break the spell *phr* /ˌbreɪk ðə 'spel/
cancer *n* /'kænsə/ ***
civil rights movement *n* /ˌsɪvl 'raɪts ˌmuːvmənt/
conversation starter *n* /ˌkɒnvə'seɪʃn ˌstɑːtə/
democratic rule *n* /ˌdeməkrætɪk 'ruːl/
donation *n* /dəʊ'neɪʃn/ ***
ease sb's guilty conscience *expr* /ˌiːz ... ˌgɪlti 'kɒnʃəns/
entire *adj* /ɪn'taɪə/ ***
equality *n* /ɪ'kwɒləti/ **
eradicate poverty *phr* /ɪˌrædɪkeɪt 'pɒvəti/
express solidarity *phr* /ɪkˌspres ˌsɒlɪ'dærəti/
fashion accessory *n* /'fæʃn əkˌsesəri/ **
from top to bottom *expr* /frəm ˌtɒp tə 'bɒtəm/
give money to charity *phr* /ˌgɪv ˌmʌni tə 'tʃærəti/
go mad *expr* /ˌgəʊ 'mæd/
immaculate *adj* /ɪ'mækjʊlət/
injustice *n* /ɪn'dʒʌstɪs/
jump on (the) bandwagon *expr* /ˌdʒʌmp ɒn (ðə) 'bændˌwægən/
make an exception *phr* /ˌmeɪk ən ɪk'sepʃn/
military ruler *n* /ˌmɪlɪtri 'ruːlə/
non-violent protest *n* /ˌnɒn ˌvaɪələnt 'prəʊtest/
peace *n* /piːs/ ***
physical *adj* /'fɪzɪkl/ ***
poverty *n* /'pɒvəti/ **
racism *n* /'reɪsɪzm/ *
raise awareness *phr* /ˌreɪz ə'weənəs/
raise money *phr* /ˌreɪz 'mʌni/
segregation *n* /ˌsegrɪ'geɪʃn/
show commitment *phr* /ˌʃəʊ kə'mɪtmənt/
smug *adj* /smʌg/
spread the word *phr* /ˌspred ðə 'wɜːd/
stillness *n* /'stɪlnəs/
support a cause *phr* /səˌpɔːt ə 'kɔːz/
waste of time *phr* /ˌweɪst əv 'taɪm/
without doubt *phr* /wɪˌðaʊt 'daʊt/
wristband *n* /'rɪstˌbænd/

Unit 4

all down to sb *phr* /'ɔːl daʊn tə/
array *n* /ə'reɪ/ *
be rooted in *phr* /bɪ 'ruːtɪd ɪn/
by hook or by crook *expr* /baɪ 'hʊk ɔː baɪ ˌkrʊk/
cherished *adj* /'tʃerɪʃt/
come back from *phr* /ˌkʌm 'bæk frəm/
come up against *phr* /ˌkʌm 'ʌp əˌgenst/
come up with *phr* /ˌkʌm 'ʌp wɪð/
compensate for *v* /'kɒmpənseɪt fə/
dazzling *adj* /'dæzlɪŋ/
dizzying *adj* /'dɪziɪŋ/
drop out of *phr* /'drɒp ˌaʊt əv/
due to *phr* /'djuː tə/
face up to *phr* /ˌfeɪs 'ʌp tə/
fall back on *phr* /ˌfɔːl 'bæk ɒn/
fight a losing battle *phr* /ˌfaɪt ə ˌluːzɪŋ 'bætl/
get off to a flying start *expr* /get ˌɒf tuː ə ˌflaɪɪŋ 'stɑːt/
get on with *phr* /ˌget 'ɒn wɪð/
heartbroken *adj* /'hɑːtbrəʊkən/
huddle *n, v* /'hʌdl/
look up to *phr* /ˌlʊk 'ʌp tuː/
machete *n* /mə'ʃeti/
make it big *expr* /ˌmeɪk ɪt 'bɪg/
make up for *phr* /ˌmeɪk 'ʌp fə/
must-see *adj* /'mʌst ˌsiː/
overcome the odds *phr* /ˌəʊvəkʌm ði 'ɒdz/
owe everything to *phr* /ˌəʊ 'evriθɪŋ tə/
pass with flying colours *phr* /ˌpɑːs wɪð ˌflaɪɪŋ 'kʌləz/
pint-sized *adj* /'paɪnt ˌsaɪzd/
puny *adj* /'pjuːni/
put up with *expr* /ˌpʊt 'ʌp wɪð/
quick-thinking *adj* /ˌkwɪk 'θɪŋkɪŋ/
rip *v* /rɪp/ **
role model *n* /'rəʊl ˌmɒdl/ *
run out of *phr* /'rʌn ˌaʊt əv/
sail through it *phr* /'seɪl ˌθruː ɪt/
shred *v* /'ʃred/
sink or swim *expr* /ˌsɪŋk ɔː 'swɪm/
slaughter *n, v* /'slɔːtə/ *
spate *n* /speɪt/
spree *n* /spriː/
spur sb on to do sth *phr* /ˌspɜː ... ɒn tə 'duː .../
stand up for *expr* /ˌstænd 'ʌp fə/
stand up to *expr* /ˌstænd 'ʌp tə/
steal the show *phr* /ˌstiːl ðə 'ʃəʊ/
succinct *adj* /sək'sɪŋkt/
supreme *adj* /sʊ'priːm/ **
throw in the towel *expr* /ˌθrəʊ ɪn ðə 'taʊəl/
tolerate *v* /'tɒləˌreɪt/
trite *adj* /traɪt/
underdog *n* /'ʌndəˌdɒg/
win hands down *expr* /ˌwɪn ˌhændz 'daʊn/

Communication activities

Unit 2, Lead-in Ex 1 page 6

a The Acropolis, Athens, Greece.
b Alhambra, Grenada, Spain
c Angkor, Cambodia
d Colosseum, Rome, Italy
e The Statue of Liberty, New York City, USA
f Eiffel Tower, Paris, France
g The Great Wall of China, China
h Hagia Sophia, Istanbul, Turkey
i The Kremlin, St Basil's Cathedral, Moscow, Russia
j Machu Picchu, Peru
k Petra, Jordan
l The Pyramids of Giza, Egypt
m Statues of Easter Island, Easter Island
n Sydney Opera House, Australia
o The Taj Mahal, Agra, India

Unit 2, Listening and vocabulary Ex 6 page 9

Student A

Rolecard

You have a lot of problems. You've just lost your job as a trainee journalist on a local newspaper because the newspaper has had to make cutbacks and you haven't got much prospect of getting another position locally. You've been feeling depressed about this and it has affected your relationship with your girlfriend / boyfriend: she / he has asked for a cooling off period as your constant moaning is getting her / him down. Losing your job also means you can't afford the rent on your new flat and will have to move somewhere smaller and cheaper. All in all, you're feeling pretty sorry for yourself and take every opportunity to tell other people how hard done by you are.
By chance you have just met Student B in the shopping centre. He / she is a school friend who you haven't seen for a long time, and you are now in a café talking. Tell him / her about your problems.

Unit 3, Vocabulary and speaking Ex 4 page 13

Read the rolecard and prepare your arguments.

Rolecard

You're collecting money for children orphaned by AIDS in Africa. They need money for food, health care and education and you also want to raise awareness in Africa about AIDS. You knock at Partner B's door. Convince him / her to give money by appealing to his / her conscience.

Unit 5, Speaking Ex 2 page 20

The category winners were: Communications – World Wide Web, Household – electric light, The arts and music – the piano, Transport – bicycle

Unit 5, Song Ex 3 page 21

'*Suddenly I See* is about the fact that singer Patti Smith looks great on the cover of her record *Horses* and I wanted to be like that.' (KT Tunstall)

Listening scripts

Unit 1 Behave!

Listening script 01

Reading text from page 3

Listening script 02

Vocabulary and speaking Ex 1 from page 2

Listening script 03

(T= Teacher, A= Alex, a student from Germany, M= Mette, a student from Denmark, N= Natsuko, a student from Japan)

T: Right, we're going to talk a bit about nonconformism. Er … Alex, what about you? Are you a nonconformist? Do you follow society's rules for behaviour, dress and things like that, or don't you care what other people think of you?

A: Er, well, I suppose I'm quite conventional really. I don't think I deliberately try to be different for the sake of it. In some ways I don't actually want to stand out. Probably because I'm too lazy. I think you have to have time to think about projecting an alternative image. You have to, er, work at being different. I'm not bothered about standing out from the crowd.

T: Is it difficult to be a nonconformist in Germany?

A: Well, it depends where you live. Germany's such a big country. If you live in a small village in the south, I don't think people perhaps are as tolerant about people being different. But I come from Berlin so for me …

M: Berlin? Great city!

A: Er, yeah, … Anyway, in a big city like Berlin there are lots of people from different countries, and lots of different lifestyles. There's no one norm that everyone follows, so it's harder to say what conformism and nonconformism is. On the whole, German people are quite individual and …

M: That reminds me of a trip I took to er Berlin last year. I was just amazed, you know, how individual people were there, everybody looked so different. In my town people all dress the same way.

T: So is there a lot of pressure to conform in Denmark, then, Mette?

M: Definitely. It's a small country and it's like, everybody thinks the same. People tend to do everything in groups. In kindergarten, you have to have the whole class to your birthday and then in school you have to do endless cooperative projects. If you don't like spending time with other people, you've had it, you don't fit in and er …

N: Sorry to interrupt, but, Denmark sounds a lot like Japan with the group … er … mentality, you know. We have a saying in Japanese, in English it's something like 'The nail that sticks out gets hammered down …'. People don't like you being different. You're made to conform in school and at work.

A: I've never … er … been to Japan but I've seen some Japanese TV shows on TV in Germany. They're wild, there's just no limits to what people do on those shows. That doesn't fit with conformism.

M: And you look quite unconventional, don't you? You know your clothes and …

N: Wait a minute! Just because I like wearing unusual clothes doesn't mean I'm a nonconformist. In fact in Tokyo I don't look 'unconventional'! All my friends dress like this. I think …

A: And don't people in Japan …

N: Just let me finish, please. I think nonconformism has more to do with personality and how you view other people.

M: Yeah, you have to be very tolerant towards other people and also be quite thick-skinned yourself … To get back to what I was saying before, I like doing things by myself. I've always liked doing my own thing. I suppose other people would say I'm a loner. Some people say I'm stuck up. A lot of people don't like it if you don't follow the crowd. They feel threatened somehow.

A: Talking of threatening situations …

Unit 2 Form and function

Listening script 04

Reading text from page 7

Listening script 05

(K=Kyle, N=Nicola)

K: Hello, 6431845?

N: Hi Kyle. How's it going?

K: Oh, hi Nicola. It's going OK but I'm getting a bit sick of sitting at my desk every day. This isn't what I expected working at home would be like!

N: Come on, it can't be that bad. This is your dream job, remember? No 9 to 5, no boss, no boring meetings … I bet you're still in your pyjamas right now watching the daytime soaps!

K: Yeah, I wish! I've got so much work I don't even have time to have lunch, let alone watch TV. I'm just up to my eyes in paper and more paper. I can't see my desk for work.

N: Oh, poor you! But I suppose that's good news, isn't it? It means your company is doing well.

K: Yes, it is. I've been inundated with great projects, which is, pretty amazing after such a short time … it usually takes a while to get the quality of work I've been getting, so of course, I'm really pleased it's worked out … I just never realised how little time I'd have. Basically I'm just at work all the time – all day and then usually most of the evening as well. But I must admit, I miss the drinks after work with the lads and the office gossip. I felt I saw my colleagues a bit too much outside work when I had my office job, but now I'm fed up with being on my own and looking at the same four walls all day.

N: Well, I can imagine it's a bit lonely at times. I certainly want a job where I work with other people. Perhaps not in an office, but definitely with other people … But, Kyle, you must talk to people on the phone, at least?

K: Sometimes, of course. But most people do business by email. I know it's cheaper than phoning but it's just so anonymous. And people send me mails about every little thing. I get a new email every ten minutes and it's driving me mad. I just can't get anything done.

N: Oh dear, I'm sorry. I thought you'd be happy working for yourself at home. You certainly whinged enough about your office job!

K: Yeah, I suppose on balance, working at home is still better than working in an office. It's great that I decide what I do with my time rather than someone else – even if I do end up deciding to work all the time … Anyway, sorry, Nicola, I know I'm being a pain in the neck going on like this. I'll stop moaning now!

N: Well, the good news is I'm coming up to the city tomorrow. So cheer up! You can take me out for a drink – just pretend I'm one of the lads!

Unit 3 It's up to you!

Listening script 06

It was my sister who got tickets for the Live 8 concert in London – one of the concerts that Bob Geldof organised for 'Make Poverty History'. She thought it might cheer me up because I'd had a terrible year and I was feeling a bit depressed. Yeah, so there we were in Hyde Park, and the sun was blazing down and this vast crowd of people was chilling out, enjoying the music and, there was a … a great feeling, really laid-back. Everyone on stage was talking about the message, the meaning of … of the concert, that it was a political event not a party. The crowd was lapping it all up but the speeches rang a bit hollow to me somehow.

But, then … er … Bob Geldof came on stage and he … er … sang one of my favourite songs, *I don't like Mondays*. It was magical. And with him up there singing on stage, the mood in the crowd seemed to intensify. There was this fantastic buzz, a feeling that this was a very special day … that … that something momentous was taking place. It was as if anything was possible, that music really could change the world, you know. It's hard to describe now, such a long time after the event, and it's probably even harder to understand what it was like if you weren't there. It was like everyone's hope was embodied in this one man. The whole crowd was on a high. And then I just realised that my own experiences were so … so trivial, compared to what's happening in other parts of the world. I failed my exams and broke up with my boyfriend – well, so what? People are dying of hunger, it's things like that that are important. You can't just live your life for yourself, everyone has a responsibility to other people. I know it sounds, well, trite, now, when I put it like that, but it was an absolute revelation to me then, at that moment in time. That day was a huge turning point in my life.

Listening script 07

1 I just couldn't believe it. I was totally speechless.

2 It was so good to see them again after all that time, you know.

3 It was a complete shock. I had no idea what they'd been planning, at all.

4 It took us an absolute age to get to the top, but it was well worth it. The views were absolutely stunning.

5 The whole day was amazing, from start to finish. It was even better than I'd dared imagine.
6 It was without doubt the single best moment of my entire life.

Listening script 08

Reading texts from page 12

Unit 4 No pain, no gain

Listening script 09

Reading text from page 15

Listening script 10

Max
What motivates me? Well, I think my motivation is rooted in my childhood. I was an only child and my parents thought everything I did was fantastic. For example, when I built something with building blocks, they'd praise me so much you'd think I'd built the Taj Mahal! And when we played games, they always let me win hands down and told me how clever I was. My confidence today is definitely due to the way I was brought up. And today I'd have to say that it's still praise that motivates me to do things. The downside is, though, that I just can't put up with criticism. I try not to show it but even the slightest hint of negativity makes me feel quite vulnerable.

Chloe
Last year I was feeling quite depressed. The stupid thing was that there was no particular reason for it. I'd passed my exams with flying colours and had started college, training to be a physiotherapist, my dream job. And I just felt so down. Maybe it was the anti-climax after studying so hard for exams and the high of getting through them. But suddenly I just couldn't see a reason to get out of bed in a morning. Then … well, I hate to admit this because it sounds so corny, but I was encouraged to get on with my life after seeing Kylie Minogue on TV. It was just after she'd had breast cancer, she'd been through chemotherapy and lost her hair. And suddenly there she was in New York looking so full of life. And I thought: 'What's up with you? If she can get on with life, you can'. So I really made an effort and now I feel great. And it's all down to Kylie!

Tom
My motivation? Well, I haven't always been as motivated as I am now. My parents are real high-fliers. They're both architects. They always put pressure on me to do well at school and they were quite disappointed that I was just average. Anyway, when I was 16, I decided to throw in the towel at school. I suppose you could say failure forced me to do something different. I dropped out of school – much to my parents' disappointment – and I concentrated on what I really enjoyed: art. I'm a freelance artist now. To be honest, I don't think I'll ever make it big as an artist, but I love what I'm doing – and that spurs me on to try and be better. And because my parents can see I'm happy, they've accepted what I do and are even quite proud of the fact that I stood up for what I wanted.

Ellen
I know I'm going to be successful simply because I know I can achieve whatever I want to achieve. And I think this is because, er, all my life I've had a very strong role model. My mother got divorced when I was two and was left to look after three small children on her own. She also worked part-time as a doctor. When I was older, my mum told me she knew it was a sink or swim moment in her life. And she didn't want to sink, she wanted to show everybody she could manage her family life and be successful at the same time. She was just determined to do it, you know – by hook or by crook. I've sort of inherited the same … er, determination and strong belief in myself. I owe everything to my mum.

Unit 5 Review

Listening script 11

(SP = Presenter, P = Paul, A = Alex, C = Chris)

SP: While most of his fellow students were already running out of what little cash they had during fresher's week, Nottingham University student Alex Tew made over £100,000. The 21-year-old undergraduate then went on to net more than a million dollars during his first term at university. So what was the secret of Alex's sudden wealth? Our business correspondent Paul Benn takes up the story.

P: Alex Tew came up with the idea one night in August 2005 while he was contemplating the financial consequences of starting a university course. The fees and accommodation for the first year alone were starting to look daunting and with no finances to fall back on Alex was dreading running up huge debts. As Alex tells us himself …

A: I've always been an ideas sort of person and I like to brainstorm at night before I go to sleep – it's my most productive time. So I wrote down 'How can I become a millionaire before I go to university?' It was a rather ambitious question, but I went with it. Then I wrote down the attributes that this idea would need: it had to be simple to understand and to set up; it had to attract a lot of media interest: and it needed a good name. After I wrote down those three things, the idea just popped into my head. I'd like to say it was more dramatic than that, but it wasn't.

P: Alex's idea was to design a web page consisting of exactly one million pixels, the dots which make up a computer screen, and to sell those pixels as advertising space, costing a dollar per pixel. Clicking on that space would take you to the buyer's website. Alex immediately got on with setting up the website and he bought the domain name 'milliondollarhomepage.com' that same evening. To get things up and running, he sold his first block of 100 pixels, which is the minimum number the eye can read, to his brothers and some friends. He then used that money to pay for a press release and that's when the site really took off. Advertisers were attracted to it by its novelty and by the curiosity factor, and with people flocking to take a look at the website that made the advertising good value for money. Chris Magras, Chief Executive of engineseeker.com, an Arizona-based company, bought 6,400 pixels as soon as he heard about the Million Dollar Homepage.

C: It was ingenious. It is easy to make money on the Internet, but it is very difficult to have a unique idea, and this was. The results for us were amazing. We used to get 40,000 visitors a day to our site – that's now up to 60,000.

P: And back in his student digs, when he wasn't catching up with course work or attending lectures, Alex managed to keep track of the money rolling in, which it did at the rate of tens of thousands of pounds per week. And not for one minute did Alex consider dropping out of university. And in a final typically inventive money-spinning twist, Alex sold the last 1000 pixels for 38 times their face value via an ebay auction at the beginning of his second university term. As seems to be the norm with internet-based business, the Million Dollar Homepage rapidly spawned hundreds of copycat sites, but none were anywhere near as successful as Alex's. Experts agree that the Million Dollar Homepage's success is down to three things: the power of word of mouth, that it's the rags-to-riches story of an ordinary student, and that it was a truly innovative yet simple idea. Expect to hear more from Alex Tew in the near future.

Listening script 12

Song from page 21

Communication activities

Unit 2, Listening and vocabulary Ex 6 page 9

Student B

Rolecard

You've just met Student A, an old school friend who you haven't seen for a long time, in the shopping centre and invited him / her for a cup of coffee to catch up on old times. You ask how Student A is doing. You are sympathetic at first, but gradually get annoyed at his / her attitude.

Unit 2, Reading and speaking Ex 1 page 9

1 Calculate your score and read the analysis. Compare your answers with a partner. Do you agree with the analysis?
2 Work in small groups. What do you think is the ideal workspace?
3 Present your ideas to the rest of the class.

Quiz score

1	a 1	b 5	c 3
2	a 5	b 3	c 1
3	a 1	b 5	c 3
4	a 5	b 3	c 1
5	a 3	b 1	c 5

Analysis

20+: You're conscientious and you're good at getting things sorted out. However, you're cautious when it comes to making big changes or decisions and can be inflexible. Learn to loosen up and let your creative side take over.

10–19: You have a balanced attitude to work: you get things done but you're not chained to your workspace. When it comes to other areas of your life, though, you may sit on the fence. Take opportunities with both hands – and don't think too much about the consequences.

5–9: You pride yourself on your individuality and a stimulating, creative workspace is important to you. But your creativity may be getting in the way of your efficiency. Clear up and try not to get distracted from the real issues.

Unit 3, Vocabulary and speaking Ex 4 page 13

Read the rolecard and prepare your arguments.

Rolecard

Somebody is collecting money for charity. You never give money to charities because you think it's the government's job to supply aid. You also think giving money isn't a good idea. People need to be trained to help themselves. It is more important to provide help with learning skills and professional competence.

Unit 4, Language study Ex 3 page 16

The complete quotations are as follows:

1 Too many people run out of ideas long before they run out of words. *Anonymous*
2 If your children look up to you, you've made a success of life's biggest job. *Anonymous*
3 I take a simple view of life: keep your eyes open and get on with it. *Sir Laurence Olivier, actor*
4 The way I see it, if you want the rainbow, you gotta put up with the rain. *Dolly Parton, singer*
5 It takes a great deal of courage to stand up to your enemies, but even more to stand up to your friends. *JK Rowling, author*
6 You need to feel good about yourself. The motivation has to come from within. You have nobody to fall back on except yourself. *Dana Hill, actress*

Unit 5, Speaking Ex 4 page 20

The overall winner was the bicycle.

Unit 5, Game Ex 1 page 20

Answers for the game are as follows:
Correct sentences, numbers 1, 4, 5, 7, 9, 11, 15, 16, 19, 22, 24, 26, 27, 29

Incorrect sentences and correct answers as follows:
2 She's a bit of a loser. 3 I really look up to her. 6 He's rather unorthadox. 8 It was must-watch TV. 10 She's got a vivid imagination. 12 They are fighting a losing battle. 13 It's very brightly coloured. 14 He followed in his father's footsteps. 17 It's badly made. 18 He did a lot to spread the word. 20 It's got an oval-shaped window. 21 They ran out of good ideas. 23 It's not very child-friendly. 25 He did a lot for civil rights. 28 He's an obsessive collector. 30 I passed with flying colours.

Module 2
Pairs

Unit	Topic	Language study	Vocabulary	Main skills
1 **Telling tales** pages 34–37	• A chance encounter (extract from *An equal music*) • The end of a nightmare (extract from *A goat's song*)	• Connecting events using the perfect	• Feelings (nouns and adjectives) • Books and reading	• **Reading:** speculating about and analysing key features of a literary text • **Speaking:** describing emotions; discussing literary texts; talking about books and reading • **Listening:** identifying key information and key features of a literary narrative • **Writing:** a short narrative
2 **A perfect world** pages 38–41	• Seeking perfection (designer babies) • Nobody's perfect (perfectionists)	• Focusing attention on important information	• Collocations: discussion issues • Phrasal verbs: debate and discussion • Phrases to express surprise or indifference	• **Reading:** understanding key information and text structure • **Speaking:** discussing genetic engineering and other current affairs topics; talking about perfection and perfectionists; expressing surprise and indifference • **Writing:** a short article • **Listening:** identifying key information • **Pronunciation:** stress and intonation when expressing surprise and indifference
3 **Modern-day icons** pages 42–45	• Keeping a legend alive (a tribute artist, nostalgia) • How star-struck are you?	• Spoken phrases with *say* and *speak*	• Idioms with parts of the body	• **Listening:** understanding gist and key information • **Speaking:** talking about popular icons and celebrity culture; discussing the value of nostalgia; using spoken phrases • **Pronunciation:** American English • **Reading:** understanding key information; completing a quiz and discussing the analysis
4 **Safe and sound?** pages 46–49	• Identity theft • Caught on camera (video surveillance)	• Using modals to express real and unreal past situations	• Banking • Expressing certainty and drawing conclusions	• **Reading:** understanding and identifying key information; understanding vocabulary in context • **Speaking:** talking about identity theft and other crimes; giving advice and warnings; using the language of banking; discussing video surveillance • **Writing:** website tips • **Listening:** identifying gist; understanding vocabulary in context

PAIRS

1 Telling tales

LEARNING AIMS

- Can discuss literary texts
- Can connect events using the perfect
- Can write a fictional narrative using dramatic and descriptive effects

1

2

3

4

Lead-in

1 What do you know about the famous couples in the photos?

2 What other famous couples can you think of? Think about contemporary couples, couples in history, and couples in literature and films.

A chance encounter

Reading and speaking

1 13 Read the novel extract on page 35 from *An equal music* by the contemporary Indian-born novelist Vikram Seth. Did you enjoy reading it? What impact did the extract have on you? Note down adjectives which describe how it made you feel.

2 Work with a partner. Speculate about the extract. Refer to the text to support your ideas.

1. Where does this extract take place?
2. How do the characters feel when they see each other on the bus?
3. What is / was their relationship?
4. How do you think the narrator feels at the end of the extract?

3 Find examples of these features in the text and discuss the effect they create with the class.

- short sentences
- the present simple used for narrative
- repetition
- descriptive verbs

4 What did you think of the outcome of this encounter? Would you have preferred a different outcome?

5 What do you think happens in the novel after this meeting? Write a paragraph explaining how you think the story of Michael and Julia ended.

Vocabulary

1 Look at the words in the table. Add the missing nouns or adjectives. Then check in the text on page 35.

Feelings	alarm	desperation					annoyance	
How you feel	*alarmed*		hesitant	astonished	dismayed	perplexed		hopeful

2 What feelings in Ex 1 do these sentences express?

1 Oh no! What have I done?
2 What the hell did you do that for?
3 Even if he hasn't rung, I think he'll turn up later.
4 Yes, I'm afraid it's true. She isn't coming.
5 I'm not sure I want to get back together with her.
6 What are you talking about? I don't understand.
7 Really? Are you absolutely sure about that?
8 You have to help me! I don't know what to do.

3 Find synonyms for the adjectives in Ex 1.

4 Look at the example situations in the box. Think of similar situations, or other situations where you have experienced some of the feelings in Ex 1. Tell a partner.

a friend lied to you   you broke or lost a valuable item   you got an unexpected text message or email   you had a job interview   you won something

Example:
I was quite hesitant about meeting my girlfriend's parents for the first time last week.

An equal music

In the bus directly opposite, at the window directly opposite is Julia. Her bus has stopped at the traffic light.

I begin to pound the window and shout, 'Julia! Julia! Julia! Julia!'

She cannot hear me. We are in separate worlds.

Stop reading, Julia. Look. Look out of the window. Look at me. Oh God.

Around me the passengers stop talking. In the bus opposite no one seems to notice. I keep pounding the window. At any moment her bus or mine could move off.

A man sitting behind her notices me and the commotion that has resulted. He looks mystified but not alarmed. I gesticulate and point desperately – and with great hesitation, he taps Julia on the shoulder and points at me.

Julia looks at me, her eyes opening wide in what? Astonishment? Dismay? Recognition? I must look wild – my face red – my eyes filled with tears – my fists still clenched – I am a decade older.

I rummage around in my satchel for a pen and a piece of paper, write my telephone number in large digits and hold it against the glass.

She looks at it, then back at me, her eyes full of perplexity.

Simultaneously both buses begin to move.

My eyes follow her. Her eyes follow me.

I look for the number that's on the back of the bus. It is 94.

I get to the stairs. I am given a wide berth. The conductor is coming up the stairs. I can't get past him. I am losing time, I am losing it.

Finally I get down, push my way past a couple of people, and jump off the moving bus.

Weaving across the traffic, I get to the other side. I have lost too much time. Her bus has moved away. I try to push through the crowd, but it is too thick. I will never catch up.

A taxi lets out a passenger. A young woman, her hands full of shopping, is about to grab it, when I interpose myself. 'Please,' I say. 'Please.'

She takes a step back and stares at me.

I get into the cab. To the taxi-driver I say: 'I want to catch up with the Number Ninety-Four in front.'

We move forward. The lights turn yellow against us. He stops.

'Couldn't you go through?' I plead. 'It's not red yet.'

'I'll get my licence taken away,' he says, annoyed. 'What's the hurry anyway? You won't save much time.'

'It's not that,' I blurt out. 'There's someone on that bus I haven't seen for years. I've got to catch it.'

'Take it easy, mate,' says the driver. But he tries his best.

After one more tricky feat of overtaking the driver says: 'Look mate, I'm nearer but, to be quite honest, I won't make it. Your best bet now is to get out and run for it.'

'You're right. Thanks.'

'That's two pounds sixty.'

I only have a five-pound note in my wallet. I tell him to keep it and grab my satchel.

I know I have no chance against the crowds on the pavement. My one hope is to run between the opposing streams of traffic.

Sweating, diesel-gassed, unable to see clearly through my most inconvenient tears, I run and gasp and run.

I catch up with the bus a little before Oxford Circus. I try to run up the stairs but can't. I walk up slowly, in hope and in dread.

Julia is not there. I go to the very front and look back at every face. I go downstairs, I look at every face. She is not there.

LANGUAGE STUDY

Connecting events using the perfect

1 What is the function of the present perfect in these extracts from the text on page 35.

1 *In the bus directly opposite, at the window directly opposite is Julia. Her bus **has stopped** at the traffic light.*

2 *Weaving across the traffic, I get to the other side. I **have lost** too much time. Her bus **has moved** away.*

3 *There's someone on that bus I **haven't seen** for years. I've got to catch it.*

2 Look at these sentences and answer the questions.

a *They'**d been chatting** all night and **had lost** all sense of time.*

b *We'**ll have been** together for two years next month.*

c *We'**ve been seeing** a lot of each other lately. I'd say we'**ve become** quite close.*

1 What is the name of each the perfect tenses in the sentences?

2 What is the function of each perfect tense in the sentences?

3 Which form, simple or continuous, do you generally use with the perfect to emphasise a) activity or duration and b) completion or result?

Grammar reference page 58

3 Complete the first part of the article by putting the verbs into an appropriate perfect form. Where both simple or continuous are possible, what is the difference in emphasis?

Bad habits can ruin *romance*

Fiddling with the controls of the car stereo or stealing chips from your partner's plate may seem minor niggles but they could ruin a relationship. Researchers, who over the last few months (1 delve) ______________ into the private lives of 500 couples, (2 identify) ______________ a list of the most annoying habits that can cause rifts between couples. One couple even split up after one partner (3 finally / have) ______________ enough of publicly being referred to as 'honeybunny' or 'bunnyboo'.

The study (4 find) ______________ that the smallest of irritations can provoke the most extreme of reactions in a partner. 'We (5 look) ______________ at how relatively minor behavioural quirks can affect a partner's emotions,' said researcher Mike Harold, 'While bickering (6 always / be) ______________ a natural feature of relationships, over time minor irritations can sometimes take on unmanageable proportions and it's possible that by then the behaviour in question (7 become) ______________ a major issue in the relationship.' 'Irritating habits (8 come up) ______________ a lot recently as an issue in relationship problems,' said therapist Philippa Hills, from YouRelate. 'Over the last couple of years we (9 see) ______________ more and more couples who (10 develop) ______________ issues concerning each other's habits.'

4 Complete the rest of the article using an appropriate perfect form of these verbs.

be do get know lose remind

Couples generally agree that finding their other half annoying is part of life. John Mitchell, 29, said of his girlfriend Susan Thomas, 'It's a mystery how she can take so long to get ready. She always (1) ______________. And I get very frustrated with her map reading. I (2) ______________ count of the number of times she (3) ______________ us lost.' John of course has his faults too according to Susan. 'He always leaves his clothes lying around, even though I (4) ______________ him about it a thousand times,' she says. Nevertheless, the couple, who next month (5) ______________ together for five years, say they are still blissfully happy. 'Even if we (6) ______________ about each other's annoying habits before we got together, we'd still have done so,' Susan added.

5 What do you think are the top ten most annoying habits according to the research in Ex 3? Turn to page 61 to find out. Which of the habits do you, or would you, find annoying?

The end of a nightmare

Listening

1 14 Listen to the first part of an extract from Dermot Healy's *A goat's song*. Choose the correct answers.

Main character: *male / female* Background: *start / break up* of a relationship

Mood: *hope / desperation* Setting: *urban / rural*

The main character's work: *farmer and fisherman / author and fisherman*

2 15 Listen to the second part of the extract and make notes about what happens.

- Work with a partner. Tell the story to your partner in your own words, using your notes. Your partner listens and points out any differences from his / her notes.
- Discuss the ending of the story – is it a happy one?

3 Use a dictionary to check the meaning of these literary techniques.

alliteration	metaphor	simile	use of a highly descriptive adjective / verb

4 Match the phrases in **bold** from the listening script, with the techniques in Ex 3.

1 He knew, with a sense of **furious sadness**, that this would be followed by another minute.

2 On the radio various voices of other fishermen were **cajoling, complaining, cursing**, talking of the forthcoming storms.

3 Her voice, filled with static, **cut through** the quiet.

4 A sound **like a strimmer** went through the airwaves.

5 He **threw open** the door of the lightkeeper's house.

6 I'm trusting you, **treading on thin ice** in the hope that someday we'll be **skating along** without fear.

Literature and you

Speaking and vocabulary

1 Do you enjoy reading for pleasure? Do you read mainly for college or work? What do you read or have to read? Tick the words in the lists. Then tell a partner.

Fiction: chick lit, classics, detective stories, historical novels, modern fiction, poetry, thrillers.

Non-fiction: blogs, chat room discussions, biographies / autobiographies, cookery books, daily or weekly newspapers, guidebooks, magazines, professional journals or articles, self-help manuals, message boards, textbooks.

2 Tell a partner about something memorable you have read recently. Use these words and phrases to help you.

a load of rubbish	a real tearjerker	a slow-starter	badly written	controversial	
disappointing	entertaining	hilarious	in-depth	informative	inspiring
monotonous	moving	poetic	superficial	trashy	unputdownable

Writing

1 You are going to write a 300–400 word short story for a competition. Choose one of these titles: A chance encounter, The end of a nightmare

2 Make notes for your story. You can draw on your own experiences if you wish. Think about the key events, the main characters' feelings and relationships, and how the story ends.

3 Write your story. Then read other students' stories. Say what you enjoyed, what could be improved on and how they made you feel.

CD-ROM For more activities go to **Pairs Unit 1**

2 A perfect world

LEARNING AIMS

- Can focus attention on important information
- Can comment on current affairs
- Can express surprise or indifference

▲ Dolly, 1996–2003

Seeking perfection

Lead-in

1 How did this sheep bring scientists 'closer to perfection'? Check your ideas on page 61.

Reading and vocabulary

1 Replace the underlined phrases with phrases from the box. Make any changes necessary.

cause concern	create controversy	inspire sympathy	make headlines
rekindle debate	set a precedent		

1 What has renewed discussion about genetic screening?
2 Why did Adam Nash's birth become a big newspaper story?
3 What aspect of the case aroused compassion?
4 Why has the case given rise to worry?
5 This is the first case of its kind. What is its importance for future cases?
6 How did a US entrepreneur provoke debate and disagreement?

2 **16** Read the article on page 39 and answer the questions in Ex 1.

3 Discuss these questions with your class.

1 Did reading about this case inspire sympathy in you or cause concern? Why?
2 Do you know if the topic of genetic screening has also created controversy in your country? If so, what has been the outcome of the discussion?
3 Plastic surgery is widely used today. To what extent is selling the embryos of models a logical further step?
4 What do you think would be 'perfect offspring'?
5 Is it possible to achieve perfection? Is it a worthwhile goal?

4 How do you think the debate on genetic screening will pan out? Does the responsibility for the use of genetic screening lie with scientists, parents or governments?

5 Work with a partner. Look at the questions and the content of each paragraph of the text on page 39. Identify the purpose of each paragraph. For example: *Paragraph 1 introduces and summarises the controversy*. Compare your ideas and establish a structure model.

6 Read this article about a report on genetically modified foods. Choose the correct meaning of the underlined phrasal verbs.

GM food has made headlines again. The renewed focus on GM foods has (1) come about because of new evidence concerning the approval of seven GM foods by the European Commission. A new report by the environmental groups *Friends of the Earth* and *Greenpeace* (2) spells out the uncertainty surrounding the dangers of GM foods. The report also (3) touches on the fact that lack of data means that certain issues relating to GM foods, such as the risk of cancer and allergies, haven't been studied at all. According to the report, the Commission (4) played down the risks and approved the foods, despite not (5) ruling out the possibility that a study to support their decision was scientifically flawed. Given the high emotions surrounding this issue, the controversy is unlikely to (6) die down in the near future.

1 happened / continued
2 hints / clearly explains
3 mentions / ignores
4 emphasised / minimised
5 dismissing / acknowledging
6 become more intense / become less intense

7 How do you feel about the growing of genetically modified crops?

Designer **babies**

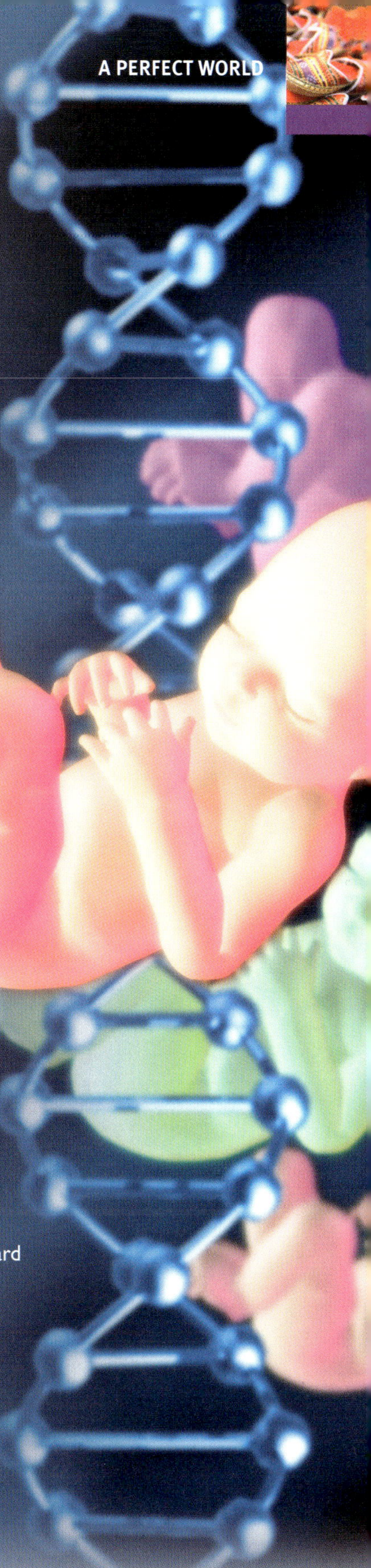

1 The first 'designer baby' has rekindled furious debate about the ethical issues of using genetics to select the attributes of babies. Genetic screening was used so that the test-tube baby Adam Nash could become a donor for his six-year-old sister Molly, who has a rare and fatal genetic disease. But whilst the case has inspired sympathy, it has also increased fears of babies becoming 'commodities' where intelligence and athletic prowess are bought.

2 **What is a 'designer baby'?**
Adam Nash, whose birth in America made headlines all over the world, is the first known designer baby. What was revolutionary about Adam's birth was that scientists genetically selected his embryo so that he would have the right cells to save the life of his dying sister. Normally, there would be a very high chance that any baby Adam's parents had would also have the disease. After Adam's birth, he became a donor to his sister and there was a blood transfusion which has more than doubled her survival chances.

3 **If he saves his sister's life, why the concern?**
Although the parents' dilemma inspired sympathy, there are those who believe it is intrinsically wrong to bring a human being into the world for any purpose other than living their own life. But, in the main, it is the precedent that this birth sets that is causing concern: the technique could be extended to allow parents to 'design' children with a variety of genetic traits.

4 **What would be available to parents deciding to have a 'designer baby'?**
Eye colour, athletic ability, beauty, intelligence, height, stopping a tendency towards obesity, guaranteeing freedom from certain mental and physical illnesses. All of these could in the future be determined by genetic science. Even characteristics such as sexuality could be selected. The problem for many is that the frontiers of what is now genetically possible are being pushed back so quickly that the ethical debate can't keep up.

5 **Who are the people worried about genetics?**
Some scientists have voiced concerns, although many echo the views of Dr John Wagner, who carried out the Nash operation. He said he was just trying to save the girl's life. The anti-abortion charity, *Life*, said selecting top quality embryos was more akin to the farmyard and that one child should not be used to save the life of another. Groups worried about social injustices, and the gap between rich and poor, are also concerned about a future where the wealthy can purchase a perfect offspring. Last year, related controversy was created when a US entrepreneur started a website offering the embryos of models.

6 **How will the debate pan out?**
As the knowledge of what each gene does grows it will become possible to predict most, if not all diseases and details of other characteristics before birth. The key issue is how parents respond to the increasing possibilities that will be offered to them.

Writing

1 Think about an issue that has been the subject of debate in your country recently and make notes, using the structure model you discussed in Reading and vocabulary Ex 5.

2 Write an article about your issue, using your notes. Introduce your paragraphs with questions similar to those in the text. Use the phrases and the phrasal verbs in Reading and vocabulary Ex 1 and 6 to help you.

3 Swap articles with a partner. Ask your partner for his / her opinion and comments.

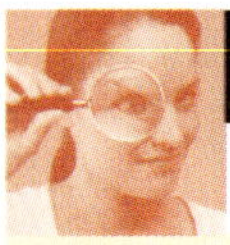

LANGUAGE STUDY

Focusing attention

1 What is the function of the phrases in **bold** in these extracts from the text on page 39?

a ***What was revolutionary about Adam's birth was*** *that scientists genetically selected his embryo so that he would have the right cells to save the life of his dying sister.*

b *But, in the main,* ***it is the precedent that this birth sets that*** *is causing concern.*

c ***The problem for many is*** *that the frontiers of what is now genetically possible are being pushed back so quickly that the ethical debate can't keep up.*

d ***The key issue is*** *how parents respond to the increasing possibilities that will be offered to them.*

2 Match the phrases in **bold** in Ex 1 with these patterns.

1 *It is / was ... that ...* ☐

2 *What ... is / was ...* ☐

3 Noun phrase + *is / was ...* ☐ ☐

Grammar reference page 58

3 Rephrase each sentence in <u>two</u> ways to focus attention more. Use (a) *It is / was ... that ...* and (b) *What ... is / was ...*

Example:
How on earth they came up with the idea in the first place amazes me.
(a) ***It's*** *how on earth they came up with the idea in the first place* ***that*** *amazes me.*
(b) ***What*** *amazes me* ***is*** *how on earth they came up with the idea in the first place.*

1 The clarity of the images amazes me.
2 What they will come up with next really frightens me.
3 I can't get my head round the distances involved.
4 Watching it live on TV really brought it home.
5 Not knowing what the long-term dangers are worries me.
6 I just don't understand how so much can be stored on something so small.

4 What phenomena could each of the sentences in Ex 3 be referring to?

5 Match the beginnings to the endings of the sentences.

1	What really irritates me about TV is	a	never having any money.
2	The best thing about the Internet is	b	all the adverts every few minutes.
3	What I'd really love is to be able to	c	the Himalayas.
4	One thing I really object to is	d	people smoking in public places.
5	The worst thing about being a student is	e	take a year off and go travelling.
6	A place I'd really love to visit is	f	their obsession with celebrity.
7	What never ceases to amaze me about the press is	g	meeting people from all over the world.
8	One thing that's great about studying English is	h	being able to download music for free.

6 Use the sentence beginnings in Ex 5 to write your own ideas. Read your sentences to a partner and discuss some of your ideas.

Example:
A: *What really irritates me about TV is all the reality shows.*
B: *Really? I think they're a bit of a laugh. They're ...*

Nobody's perfect

Listening and speaking

1 Before you listen, think about you and your parents. What have you got in common personality-wise?

2 17 Listen to the conversation. What have Ellie and her mum got in common?

3 These characteristics are typical of perfectionists. Listen again and tick the ones that apply to Ellie's mum.

1 is afraid of disapproval ☐
2 likes things to be just so ☐
3 is fussy ☐
4 is extremely competitive ☐
5 is self-critical ☐
6 has high expectations ☐
7 is indecisive ☐
8 is intolerant of mistakes ☐

4 Work with a partner. Look at the list of characteristics in Ex 3.

1 Do you know people who are perfectionists and have the characteristics in Ex 3? What positive traits do they have?
2 Do any of the things in Ex 3 apply to you? Are you a perfectionist?
3 Extreme perfectionists can suffer from illnesses such as depression, eating disorders, and addictions such as alcoholism. Why do you think this is so?

Vocabulary and pronunciation

1 How does Zoe react …

1 … when she finds Ellie hoovering?
2 … when Ellie says she might clean the fridge before she goes to bed?
How does she express these feelings? Check in the listening script on page 62.

2 Which of these phrases express surprise (S)? Which express indifference (I)? Mark them.

1	You're kidding me, aren't you?	6	No way!
2	So what?	7	Whatever.
3	Are you having me on?	8	What?
4	Who cares?	9	If you like.
5	It doesn't matter.	10	Never!

3 18 Listen and repeat the phrases. Pay attention to stress and intonation.

4 Work with a partner. Student A look at page 61. Student B respond to student A's statements with a phrase from Ex 2 and continue the conversation. Use as many phrases from Ex 2 as possible. When student A has finished, swap roles. Student B look at page 64.

Example:
A: *I found a £20 note on the street today.*
B: *No way! Some people have all the luck. I never find anything.*
A: *Do you think I should take it to the police?*
B: *Are you having me on? Why would you want to do that?*

CD-ROM For more activities go to **Pairs Unit 2**

3 Modern-day icons

LEARNING AIMS

- Can use spoken phrases with *say* and *speak*
- Can talk about popular icons and celebrity culture
- Can contrast British and American English pronunciation

Lead-in

1 An English proverb says 'Imitation is the sincerest form of flattery'. Discuss what this means. When does it go too far?

Keeping a legend alive

Listening and speaking

1 Tribute artists and bands where singers impersonate famous performers are big business. Why do you think these acts are so popular? What age group do they appeal to? Why do you think people want to be in tribute bands?

2 19 Listen to an interview with Shawn Klush, an Elvis tribute artist. Make notes on the following:

a his expectations about the concert in Switzerland
b his feelings before going on stage
c the audience and how it affected him
d what the concert shows about Elvis and his music

3 Compare your notes with a partner. Listen again if necessary.

4 What impressions do you get of Shawn Klush? How would you describe his attitude towards his work?

5 Work with a partner and discuss these questions.

1 What do you think of Elvis and his music? Why was and is he popular?
2 Elvis is a 20th-century legend. Who else would you put in this category?
3 Think about contemporary musicians and bands. Who do you think are the icons of the early 21st century? Why?

6 The nostalgia industry at present focuses on the latter half of the 20th century. Work in groups and discuss what you think people will look back on with nostalgia from the first decade of this century. Think about, for example, music, fashion, TV shows and films, food, and household gadgets and appliances. Present your ideas to the class.

7 You're going to do a role-play. Student A look at page 61. Student B look at page 64.

8 How far did you identify with the opinions and attitude you defended in Ex 7?

Vocabulary

1 In the listening text Shawn Klush uses the phrases *it blew their minds*, and *out of the public eye*. Who or what was he referring to and what do the phrases mean? Check your ideas in the listening script on page 62.

2 Many idiomatic expressions in English use parts of the body. Can you explain the meanings of these idioms?

1 She loves to be waited on hand and foot.
2 She turns heads wherever she goes.
3 He never has a hair out of place.
4 His outrageous outfits raise a few eyebrows.
5 He puts his heart and soul into his performances.
6 She always thanks her fans from the bottom of her heart.
7 Unfortunately, success has gone to his head.
8 Her name is on everyone's lips.

3 Work with a partner and discuss these questions.

1 Think of a performer you like or admire. Do any of the expressions in Ex 2 apply to him or her?

2 Which performers can be described by the other expressions?

4 Look at these everyday expressions and match them to the situations below. How else can you state the meaning of these expressions?

a Use your head!
b Keep your fingers crossed!
c Come on, let your hair down!
d Get off my back!
e Keep your eyes open!
f You scratch my back and I'll scratch yours.

1 You've been telling a friend that he doesn't work hard enough and won't pass his exams. What does he say to you?

2 You're at a party and are a bit nervous. Your friend wants you to relax and enjoy yourself. What does she say to you?

3 You need some petrol, but there seem to be no garages for miles around. What do you say to your friend in the car?

4 Your friend is going for an important audition and asks for your support. What does she say to you?

5 You want your boyfriend to help you with some tax forms. He says he'll do it – but wants you to help him with a computer program first. What does he say to you?

6 You've just had four beers and decide to drive to a friend's. Your girlfriend stops you. What does she say?

American English

Pronunciation

1 **20** Some sounds are pronounced differently in American English and British English. Look at these words. Listen and tick whether you hear British or American English. The first one has been completed for you.

		British	American			British	American
		/ɑː/	/æ/			/ɜː/	/ɜːr/
1	last		✓	5	world		
2	chance			6	work		
		/ɒ/	/ɑː/			/eə/	/eər/
3	gosh			7	there		
4	everybody			8	swear		

2 **21** Here are some words spoken with both British and American English pronunciation. Listen and mark the sound or stress that is different in American English. Then group the words into four American English pronunciation patterns.

1 garage	6 privacy
2 tomato	7 vase
3 ballet	8 café
4 vitamins	9 student
5 new	10 semi-finalist

LANGUAGE STUDY

Spoken phrases with *say* and *speak*

1 Look at these extracts from Listening and speaking Ex 2 on page 42. Match the phrases in **bold** to their uses 1–4.

... going to a different country, (a) ***as they say,*** *you know, there's different cultures and there's different this and different that.*

For a man to be ... out of the public eye, (b) ***so to speak,*** *physically,* (c) ***let's say,*** *but how he still goes on and on ...*

We really try to work hard and er, (d) ***I've said it before and I'll say it again,*** *he had impact.*

1 to show it's the opinion of a lot of people ☐

2 to give emphasis by referring to something previously stated ☐

3 to show you have expressed something in an unusual way ☐

4 to give an example ☐

Grammar reference page 59

2 Complete each sentence using an appropriate phrase in **bold** from Ex 1. Use each phrase once.

1 The best thing about the Internet is that you've always got whatever music you want at your fingertips, ________________.

2 I can't stand techno music. I'd rather listen to, ________________, folk or jazz.

3 I personally like the album, and, ________________, 20 million people can't be wrong.

4 My favourite band? ________________, *Snow Patrol* are simply the best band ever.

3 Here are some more common phrases using *say* and *speak*. What are their uses?

1 Anyway, **as I was saying**, we really must swap some music sometime.
2 **Speaking of** great gigs, I saw the *Arctic Monkeys* when they were just starting out.
3 **Personally speaking**, I really don't see the point of tribute bands.
4 I didn't really like it at first, but **I have to say** the album's really grown on me.
5 I don't really like going clubbing. **That said**, I'd rather that than stay in all night.

4 Imagine you are having a discussion about some area of entertainment such as music, film, TV or theatre. Complete the sentences with things you might say.

Example: *I'm not a big fan of Elvis. But that said, he did have a great voice.*

1 I'm not a big fan of ... But that said ...
2 I've said it before and I'll say it again, ...
3 Speaking of great shows, ...
4 I have to say ...
5 Personally speaking, ...
6 Music, as they say, ...

5 Work in groups of three. Each student writes down any five of these phrases on a piece of paper.

As I was saying ...	As they say ...	I have to say ...	
I've said it before and I'll say it again ...	Let's say ...	Personally speaking ...	
... so to speak	Speaking of ...	That said ...	

Choose one of these topics, or a topic of your choice, to discuss. As you discuss the topic, use your phrases in an appropriate way. As you use each phrase, cross it off. The first person to use all their phrases is the winner.

celebrity	computer games	Elvis Presley	marriage	money
music	nostalgia	the Internet	tribute bands	work

6 *-speak* is used with some nouns to describe the type of language associated with a certain field. Give examples of language which could be described as:

1 business-speak 2 computer-speak 3 football-speak 4 music-speak

Example: business-speak *downsize* *overheads* *parent company*

How star-struck are you?

Reading and Speaking

1 Celebrity culture (adulation and emulation of the rich and famous) has been the subject of numerous scientific studies by psychologists. Discuss these questions.

1. Why do you think psychologists are interested in this topic? What do you think they hope to find out?
2. What dangers do you think there are in people taking an interest in celebrities to extremes?
3. To what extent do you think celebrity culture is a global phenomenon? Is star gazing a popular pastime in your country?

2 Do the celebrity culture quiz. Answer 'yes' or 'no' to each question. Then look at page 64 to work out your score and to read the analysis. Do you agree with it?

How Star-struck are you?

Do you spend all your time on the Internet reading about famous people? Are you convinced your favourite celebrity is your ideal partner? Or couldn't you care less what famous people get up to in their private lives? Take this test and find out how star-struck you are.

1. I often buy tabloid newspapers or glossy magazines if there's an interesting story about a celebrity on the cover. ___
2. I'd consider plastic surgery to emulate my favourite celebrity. ___
3. I often gossip about the exploits of celebrities with my friends. ___
4. I can't believe the stupid antics of some celebrities and the way they chuck their money about. These people have got more money than sense! ___
5. I've posted a comment to a celebrity on their website or written them a fan letter. ___
6. I'm sick of stars hanging out their dirty laundry in the media. Who cares about their endless stories of drug and alcohol abuse? ___
7. If I got a fleeting glimpse of my favourite star, I'd be in seventh heaven. ___
8. I would do something illegal for my favourite celebrity if he or she asked me. ___
9. I think most celebrities are a bunch of freeloaders. ___
10. If my favourite star died, I wouldn't think life was worth living. ___
11. I would be more inclined to buy a product if it were endorsed by a celebrity I think highly of. ___
12. I think my favourite celebrity is my soul mate. ___
13. I'm counting the days until the Oscars – I love all that red-carpet glamour. ___
14. I think some celebrities are role models; they can inspire you to realise your own potential. ___
15. A lot of so-called celebrities are not talented in the least. They're purely marketing products or the result of trashy reality TV. ___
16. I've contributed to a chatroom discussion about a celebrity that I really admire or really despise. ___

3 What's the difference between being interested in a celebrity and having an obsession with them? Give examples from the quiz. Why and how do you think interest turns to obsession?

Speaking and writing

1 Work in groups. You are going to give a presentation on the effect on celebrities of being stalked by their obsessive fans. First brainstorm ideas about what happens, and what celebrities might do in response. Include any particular cases that come to mind and make notes.

2 In your group decide on the information you are going to use for your presentation and who is going to present it. Organise your notes.

3 Make a group presentation to the rest of the class. Encourage other groups to comment on or discuss your presentation.

CD-ROM For more activities go to **Pairs Unit 3**

4 Safe and sound?

LEARNING AIMS

- Can talk about real and unreal past situations
- Can discuss crime prevention and civil liberties
- Can give advice and warnings

Identity theft

Lead-in

1 Work with a partner. What do you think is private information and what should be publicly available – to authorities and companies, for example? Make two lists using the ideas in the box and your own ideas. Then compare your ideas with the class.

club membership	credit history	criminal record	date of birth
email address	medical history	political affiliation	profession
qualifications	religion	salary	school records and reports
value of your flat or house	what you read	where you shop	

Reading and vocabulary

1 What exactly is identity theft? Think about why and how it happens. Write a class definition.

2 **22** Read the information on page 47 and check your ideas from Ex 1.

3 Are these sentences true or false? Correct the false ones.

1. Financial fraud is the main reason people commit identity theft.
2. Identity theft is an online phenomenon.
3. Victims hardly ever know the people who steal their identity.
4. It's fairly easy for criminals to get hold of your personal details.

4 Choose the correct name: Rose, Scott or both. Who …

1. had their credit card details stolen?
2. got lots of bills?
3. had their current account cleaned out?
4. had a demand for a large sum of interest?
5. uses online banking?
6. checks their bank balance regularly?

5 Explain the meaning of the underlined phrases in Ex 4.

6 Match the verbs in the box to the correct nouns. Which word can go with two nouns?

clean out	close	default on	deposit	open	pay off	take out
transfer	withdraw					

________ ________ ________	a bank account	________ ________ ________ ________	money	________ ________ ________	a loan

7 Work with a partner. Discuss these questions.

1. Have you or anyone you know ever had your credit card details stolen and used by another person?
2. Have you ever considered using or do you use online banking? What security precautions would you / do you take?
3. What do you do with old bank statements and credit card receipts?

Search

Home Search Shop Bookmarks

Protect your identity

Identity theft is the world's fastest growing crime. Identity theft is when somebody steals your personal information in order to use your bank account or credit card to withdraw money, or to open new accounts or take out loans in your name. Stealing somebody's identity can also have other motives, for example, drug trafficking or illegal immigration, but these cases are less common. Fraudsters can steal personal information in various ways:

- by phishing: counterfeiting real websites (such as a bank's) and sending people to other illegitimate websites where they have to fill in personal information
- by posing as telemarketers or bank personnel on the phone and asking for personal information
- through the use of cash machines: by noting PIN codes or by using attachments to the machines
- by hacking into commercial databases of personal information or your own personal computer
- by stealing mail or stealing bank statements and credit card receipts from your rubbish bins
- by memorizing your details in their work as shop assistants or waiters
- by being related to you! Frighteningly, 10% of fraudsters are family members.

Identity theft can happen to anybody. These two stories had happy endings – but others haven't been so lucky.

Rose's story

I was a victim of identity theft because I used a free music file-sharing program. Suddenly I was getting bills for all sorts of things and being asked to pay huge amounts of interest on a credit card I didn't even have! I was just about to start college and it couldn't have happened at a worse time. Later I found out that when I downloaded the file sharing software, I must have also downloaded a spyware program that allowed the person access to the personal information on my computer. I use online banking so all the information they needed was there. I just never imagined something like this would happen to me. I got it all sorted out in the end, but it was a complete nightmare!

Scott's story

I had my personal information stolen by a guy in our pizza delivery place. I go there quite a lot and so they've got my address and telephone number in their customer database. A few months ago some friends and I went there. I had to pay by credit card, and it turns out this guy had a skimmer – one of those gadgets which you can use to take credit card data off the magnetic strip. He downloaded the information onto his PC and used that and the customer database information to make a counterfeit credit card and then clean out my current account. It could have been worse – I haven't got much credit at the bank so he couldn't get that much money. And luckily I check my balance regularly or the whole thing might have gone undetected for weeks.

Speaking and writing

1 Look at these tips about property theft from college accommodation. The phrases in bold are used for giving formal advice and warning. Can you think of other phrases that can be used?

1 **It is recommended that you** report any crimes to the main office immediately.
2 **One simple way to prevent** things being stolen is by locking your room at all times – even when in the immediate vicinity.
3 **Avoid** leaving valuables or documents such as passports in your room.
4 **Consider** purchasing a small room safe or leave valuables at the office.
5 **Take care not to** let unknown people into the building, especially at night.
6 **Beware of** people you do not know purporting to be cleaners or other maintenance staff who require entry to your room.

2 You are going to write some tips about protecting yourself from crime for a college website. Work in two groups. One group is going to write tips about preventing being mugged and the other group is going to write tips about avoiding car crime. First brainstorm ideas in your group.

3 As a group, write your information for the website using the phrases in Ex 1 and a dictionary. Give your tips to the other group.

4 Discuss the other group's work. Comment on their ideas and language and suggest other tips if necessary.

LANGUAGE STUDY

Using modals to express real and unreal past situations

1 Look at these sentences and answer the questions.

1 Which of the modal verbs in **bold** express:
(a) 'real' situations that actually existed or happened ☐ ☐
(b) 'unreal' ideas such as speculation or deduction *1* ☐ ☐ ☐

I was just about to start college and it (1) ***couldn't have*** *happened at a worse time.*
... when I downloaded the file-sharing software, I (2) ***must have*** *also downloaded a spyware program ...*
I (3) ***should have*** *been more careful but I never imagined something like this would happen to me.*
I (4) ***had to*** *pay by credit card, but didn't think anything about it.*
It (5) ***could have*** *been worse – I haven't got much credit so he (6)* ***couldn't*** *get that much money.*
I check my balance regularly online or the whole thing (7) ***might have*** *gone undetected for weeks.*

2 Complete the rules with *real* and *unreal*.

When you express ____________ situations in the past, you use modal verb + *have* + past participle.

When you express ____________ situations in the past, the modal changes form (*can→could, will→would, must / have to→had to*)

Note: *Can* only expresses real situations. Therefore its past form is *could*, and never *can have* + past participle.

Grammar reference page 59

3 Complete these identity-related news stories using the past form of the modal verbs in the box and the verbs in brackets.

could have to must should

Who's the dummy?

A motorist has been fined $250 for driving in a high-occupancy vehicle lane with a life-size inflatable doll, which he hoped would pass as a passenger. The court heard that as there was only one 'human' in the car it (1 be) ______________ in a different lane. The court was also told that the mannequin (2 burst) ______________ at any time, 'endangering the lives of other road users.' The arresting officer also said that the driver, Jim Evans, from Richmond, Kentucky '(3 pull) ______________ the stunt on more than one occasion' as he remembered seeing the same vehicle and 'passenger' before. As well as the fine, Evans (4 hand over) ______________ the doll.

could might must

A lesson in law

A con-artist (5 not / pick) ______________ a worse building to target when a stranger he tried to scam turned out to be a senior police officer. Roberto Cubillas tried to pass himself off as an impoverished student and according to police, he (6 get away with) ______________ it had his story not been so far-fetched. Cubillas told the officer that he (7 not / pay) ______________ his university fees as he had spent the money on a family funeral. 'He (8 think) ______________ I was born yesterday,' said the officer. There was no way that Cubillas (9 know) ______________ that the building was home to several high-ranking police officers. While Cubillas (10 look) ______________ like a student, he certainly hadn't done his homework!

4 Think about a time in the past when you made a wrong decision or when things didn't work out as hoped. Work with a partner and say what you should or could have done differently and what then might have happened.

Caught on camera

Listening and vocabulary

1 The use of CCTV (closed-circuit television) cameras is being hotly debated in Britain. Are CCTV cameras used in your country? In what places do you usually find them?

2 **23** Listen to the radio phone-in and match the viewpoints to the callers. Make notes on the evidence the speakers give to support their opinions.

a It's about privacy. These cameras are just spying on us.

b CCTV surveillance is harassment. People are often misidentified.

c Cameras can help detect the people who commit crimes.

d Cameras prevent people from committing crimes.

Caller 1, Jody: ______ Caller 2, Naseem: ______ Caller 3, Lily: ______
Caller 4, Alvin: ______

3 Listen again. Note down the phrases the speakers use to express opinions. What other phrases do you know for expressing opinions?

1 I ________________ having cameras everywhere.
2 I ________________ they help stop people from committing crimes.
3 Most people ________________ that video surveillance has made them feel safer.
4 I ________________ privacy ought to be the main issue here.
5 I ________________ that we can't be expected to have faith in video surveillance.
6 I ________________ that we need CCTV.

4 Work with a partner.

1 Tell your partner which viewpoint(s) in Ex 2 you agree most with. Why? What is most important: civil liberties or public protection? Express your opinions using the phrases in Ex 3.
2 Do you think there should be restrictions on cameras in certain places – for example schools, nurseries, swimming pools? Why or why not?

5 Work with a partner. Make a mind map about crime. First use words and phrases from the listening text and the rest of the unit. Then find other important words using a dictionary.

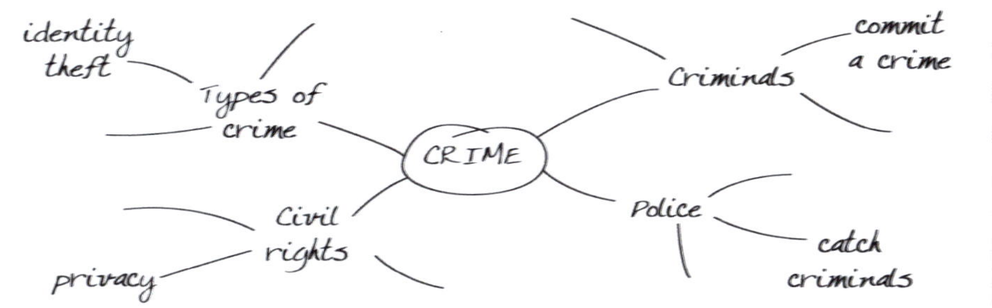

Speaking

1 The council in your town wants to introduce CCTV cameras in a neighbourhood which has had problems with theft, joyriding and mugging. Work in two groups. Group A look at page 61. Group B look at page 64. Follow the instructions.

CD-ROM For more activities go to **Pairs Unit 4**

5 Review

Lead-in **1**

1. Can you make four celebrity couples from the people in the photos? What do you know about them? Are they still together?
2. Are there any famous celebrity couples in your country?
3. Why do you think celebrities are attracted to other celebrities?
4. What do you think are the pros and cons of being a celebrity couple?

The world of celebrity

1 Choose the most natural alternative in the article.

Celebrity splits *under the spotlight*

The recent break-ups of many celebrity couples, including some of Hollywood's most bankable stars, (1) *have shown / have been showing* that relationships can and do crack under the pressures of fame and fortune. Divergent careers which constantly keep the couple apart, and the strain of heavy work schedules is often to blame. Career jealousy is another reason, especially when one partner's career (2) *has been taking off / has taken off* more than the other's. But the most likely reason is that one or the other (3) *has been meeting / has met* someone else, invariably after falling for a co-star or someone they (4) *have worked / have been working* with in some other capacity. It is a wonder how some of today's celebrity couplings (5) *have lasted / have been lasting* as long as they have.

On the other hand, stars do find it easier to date each other than members of the public. If you (6) *have drunk / have been drinking* champagne on the set all day and you come home to someone who (7) *has never lived / has never been living* in that world and talk about what a hard day you (8) *have been having / have had*, they won't understand.

2 How do your ideas in Lead-in question 4 compare with those in the article?

3 24 Listen to part of a conversation and answer these questions.

1. Which of the topics are talked about?
2. What opinions are expressed about these topics?

celebrity endorsements ☐	celebrity magazines ☐
celebrity weddings ☐	clothes ☐
earning money ☐	freebies ☐
good causes ☐	self-publicity ☐
spending money ☐	the Oscars ☐

▲ Ben and Anna

4 Complete these extracts from the listening with the correct form of *say* or *speak*. What is each commenting on?

1. *That* ____________, I do agree that it's maybe getting a little out of hand.
2. Yes, *I have to* ____________ it can be pretty gross …
3. But *as they* ____________, if you've got it, flaunt it.
4. ____________ *of* 'flaunting it', did you see those hideous pictures of …
5. They got paid a million, *or so they* ____________, by some magazine.
6. The right one on the front cover of, *let's* ____________, 'Hello' magazine … can boost sales massively.
7. *As I was* ____________, I suppose any publicity is good publicity.

5 These phrases were used by Anna to focus attention. Complete them to give your own opinions about some of the topics in the box in Ex 1.

Example: *It never ceases to amaze me that anyone should think a product is special just because it's endorsed by a celebrity.*

1 It never ceases to amaze me …
2 Another thing that really annoys me is …
3 What I don't understand is …
4 It's … that gets me.
5 And what I want to know is …

6 Complete these extracts from film reviews with the past form of an appropriate modal verb and the verb in brackets.

Example: The stunning twist at the end (be) couldn't have been more surprising.

1 This film (be) ___________ great fun to make – the entire cast seems to be relishing every moment and the movie never takes itself too seriously.

2 I wanted to stay to the end, but I just (not / bear) ___________ watching this rubbish for a moment longer. I (leave) ___________ after 20 minutes.

3 The hype surrounding this film has made seeing it a more desirable night out than it (otherwise / be) ___________. It's good, but it isn't a great movie.

4 This film is so badly made that the boom microphone (list) ___________ as a supporting character.

5 Watching with a friend we (pause) ___________ it every five minutes to check what was going on. The film (not / make) ___________ any less sense if we had been watching without sound.

7 Could any of the extracts in Ex 4 describe any films you have seen? Tell a partner.

Example: *Number one could be describing 'Pirates of the Caribbean'. The lead actor …*

8 Imagine you are a film critic. Think of three well-known films and write a short summary for each. Use at least one past modal verb in each summary.

9 Read your summaries to a partner. Can you guess what the films are?

Speaking

1 Work in two groups. You are going to have a debate. Imagine a law has been proposed to ban the paparazzi.

- Each group should choose someone to chair the debate, equal numbers of speakers for and against the proposed law, and an audience to ask questions.
- If you are one of the speakers, prepare your arguments. If you are a member of the audience prepare questions to ask the speakers.
- Hold the debate. If you are chairing the debate make sure you follow the debate procedure and make sure everyone contributes.

Debate procedure

1 The first speaker for the proposed law speaks.
2 The first speaker against the proposed law speaks.
3 Other speakers speak for and against the proposed law.
4 The audience asks the speakers questions.
5 The audience votes on the proposed law.

The paparazzi have no real career of their own, so they just make a living out of other people's.

What gets me is that celebrities are more than happy to pose for photographers when it suits them. But not at other times. They can't pick and choose.

They need us as much as we do them.

We keep them in the limelight and make them into even bigger stars.

The public has made them who they are, so they should be prepared to give something back.

The important thing to remember is that celebrities have private lives too.

They should be protected by the same privacy laws as the rest of us.

Sure we're actors, but I don't remember any of us agreeing that these people can climb over our walls and sneak around our property.

Song

1 Read the factfile about James Blunt. What connects James Blunt with the following?

Harrow School	Aerospace engineering	Sandhurst	the British Army
NATO	the Queen Mother	Los Angeles	Star Wars

2 Work with a partner and discuss these questions.

1 In what way did James Blunt follow in his father's footsteps?
2 What part did music play in his time in the army?

factfile

Singer-songwriter James Blunt was born in Wiltshire, England in 1974 and was educated at Harrow, one of the UK's top public schools. From there he gained an army-sponsored place at Bristol University, where he studied Aerospace Engineering and Sociology before finally completing his education at the Royal Military Academy in Sandhurst. Blunt's father had also been in the British Army and his family has a long history of military service.

Blunt rose to the rank of captain and served as a tank commander in the NATO peacekeeping force in Kosovo, where he carried his guitar around with him strapped to his tank and regularly entertained his fellow troops. Some of the songs from his as yet unwritten debut album were inspired by his experiences there. One of his final duties in the army was as part of the guard of honour at the funeral of the Queen Mother in 2002.

Blunt left the army in 2002 to become a full-time musician. He went to the USA and through a friend of a friend ended up in Los Angeles lodging with the *Star Wars* actress Carrie Fisher. Here he put a band together and soon afterwards he recorded his debut album, *Back to bedlam*. In 2005, the third single from the album, *You're beautiful*, was Blunt's breakthrough hit, reaching number one in several countries.

3 Match each line in the song with its final word or phrase.

4 **25** Listen and check your answers.

5 Which expressions in the song mean:

1 not worry or get upset about something?
2 suddenly notice something?
3 pass each other?
4 accept the situation?

6 Work with a partner and discuss these questions.

1 What event is he describing?
2 Who is he singing to?
3 What is his connection with this person?
4 How does he feel?

You're beautiful

My life is	subway
My love is	brilliant
I saw an	sure
Of that I'm	pure
She smiled at me on the	plan
She was with another	sleep on that
But I won't lose no	angel
'Cause I've got a	man
Chorus	
You're beautiful, you're	face
You're beautiful, it's	do
I saw your	beautiful
In a crowded	you
And I don't know what to	place
'Cause I'll never be with	true

Yeah, she caught my	moment
As we walked on	face
She could see from my	high
that I was flying	again
And I don't	eye
that I'll see her	think
But we shared a	end
that will last till the	by
Chorus	
You're beautiful, you're	you
You're beautiful, it's	angel
There must be an	beautiful
with a smile on her	true
When she thought	face
that I should be with	up
But it's time to face the	you
I will never be with	truth

Pairs 52

Vocabulary

1 Work in groups of three or four. Read how to play 'Talk about it', then play the game.

Talk about it

How to play

1 Each group needs a dice and each player needs a counter.
2 The first player rolls the dice and moves the appropriate number of squares. He / She then has to talk about the person, thing or situation described on the square for 30 seconds. Players should be timed from the moment they start talking to give them some thinking time.
3 If a player is too hesitant or repetitive, or does not speak for a full 30 seconds, he / she misses the next go. The other players act as referees.
4 The second player now plays and so on. The game continues until the first player reaches the 'finish' square.

Start

1 a time when you kept your fingers crossed	2 something which has recently created controversy	3 someone whose name is on everyone's lips at the moment	4 something currently making headlines
5 something which was a load of rubbish	6 a time when you had somebody on	7 someone who never has a hair out of place	8 a time when you really let your hair down
9 someone who turns heads wherever they go	10 something which is a cause for concern	11 a time when you were dismayed about something	12 someone whose appearance usually raises a few eyebrows
13 a time when you were too hesitant	14 something which inspires sympathy	15 a tearjerker you have read	16 something perplexing
17 a time when you were treading on thin ice	18 someone for whom success has gone to their head	19 something you are fussy about	20 a time when you needed cajoling

Finish

Extra practice

Unit 1

1 Complete the novel extracts with an appropriate form of the word in *italics*.

1. On turning the corner, Molly was ___________ to see that the damage to the house was far greater than she had expected. *dismay*
2. She turned as the car drew to a halt. The passenger door opened and she walked _______ towards it. *hesitate*
3. 'What on earth do you want to move to England for?' asked Marek in ___________. *astonish*
4. 'Please, somebody must have seen it happen,' she pleaded with more than a note of ___________ in her voice. *desperate*
5. Alfie then shut the gate and ambled off to the house, shaking his head in ___________, to complain to a ___________ Dora in the kitchen. *perplex* *sympathy*
6. Jean-Luc's head was tilted to the side, and his face was wearing an expression of ___________ and ___________. *annoy* *confuse*

2 Complete the first part of the text with an appropriate perfect tense of the verbs in brackets.

Bed sharing 'drains men's brains'

A recent study (1 find) _____________ that when a man shares a bed, his sleep is disturbed and by morning his stress hormone levels (2 rise) _____________ significantly. Women who share a bed, on the other hand, are more likely to sleep more deeply and be mentally sharper in the morning.

The study involved couples who (3 live) _____________ together for at least a year. Each couple spent some nights sleeping together and some apart. The couples decided when they slept together, as long as by the end of the research period they (4 spend) _____________ ten nights together and ten apart. The couples performed mental agility tests each morning.

Although the men reported they (5 sleep) _____________ better with a partner, they actually fared worse in the tests when they (6 do) _____________ so.

'It's not surprising that people are disturbed by sleeping together and it is actually quite bizarre that sleeping together (7 evolve) _____________ as a habit, because sleep is vital for good physical and mental health,' says Dr Neil Stanley, a sleep expert at the University of Surrey.

3 In the second part of the text, choose the most natural alternative. If both are possible, what is the difference in emphasis?

'Even though both sexes report a more disturbed night's sleep when they (1) *have shared / have been sharing* their bed, women apparently manage to sleep more deeply when they do eventually drop off, and by morning their stress hormone levels on the whole (2) *will not have increased / will not have been increasing* anything like a man's,' explained Dr Stanley. 'There is a suggestion that women (3) *have evolved / have been evolving* to cope better with broken sleep. The female brain (4) *has evolved / has been evolving* for thousands of years to cope with natural life events that involve disturbed sleep – bringing up children and tending to them in the middle of the night being one of the most obvious.'

But Dr Stanley, who (5) *has studied / has been studying* people's sleeping habits for over 20 years, added that people do get used to sharing a bed over time. 'If they (6) *have shared / have been sharing* their bed with their partner for a long time, they miss them when they are not there and that disturbs their sleep.'

4 Write about four books you have read or films you have seen that can be described by the words in the box.

a slow-starter	a tearjerker	controversial
monotonous	moving	superficial
trashy	unputdownable	

Example: *In my opinion, the Da Vinci Code was good, but a bit superficial.*

1 ______________________________
____

2 ______________________________
____

3 ______________________________
____

4 ______________________________
____

Unit 2

1 Complete the text with an appropriate form of the verbs in the box.

ban cause create govern make modify rekindle set

GM food – a quick guide

Genetically modified food is constantly (1)__________ the headlines and each latest newsworthy development (2)__________ the debate for and against it. But what exactly is GM food?

In a word, it is food that comes from plants which have had their genetic make-up (3)__________ in order to improve the yield or to enable the plant to exist in more extreme environments than non-GM crops.

The precedent for GM food was actually (4)__________ thousands of years ago when farmers first crossed similar species. However, modern GM (5)__________ concern because critics say the modified crops could cross-pollinate with wild plants, with unknown consequences.

GM supporters claim the regulations that (6)__________ GM foods are stricter than for non-GM foods and that there is no evidence that GM crops are a danger to human health. They say the benefits are that GM crops produce higher yields and therefore they are more efficient in terms of land use, and use fewer pesticides.

However, GM foods have had so much bad publicity that supermarkets in several countries have (7)__________ them. And until the scientists can agree, the only thing we can be totally sure of about GM food is that it will continue (8)__________ controversy.

2 Replace the underlined phrases in these news extracts with the correct form of the phrasal verbs in the box.

come about die down pan out play down rule out spell out touch on

1 The official line on further investment remains the same, but in reality the government is waiting to see how things develop before making a decision. ______________

2 Ministers close to the president have minimised the importance of any rift between him and the home secretary. ______________

3 Professor Wood will talk endlessly about his pioneering research, but when questions mention the political implications, however, he changes the subject. ______________

4 The decline in the number of people living in rural areas has primarily happened because of drastic changes in farming methods over the last 20 years. ______________

5 The furore over the nuclear programme will surely become less intense with time.

____

6 The government has explained clearly its policy on cloning, and while it hasn't dismissed a total ban, it has said that stricter regulations would be enforced. ______________ ______________

3 Rewrite these sentences to focus attention more.

1 Not knowing the long-term effects of GM food concerns me.

What concerns me ____________________________

2 The feeling of helplessness really frustrates me.

It's ____________________________

3 I don't understand why on earth anyone would want to live here.

What ____________________________

4 Not knowing who has got access to all your personal details on the Internet worries me.

It's ____________________________

5 Crick and Watson discovered the structure of DNA, didn't they?

Wasn't ____________________________?

4 Rearrange these sentence beginnings.

1 is / about / thing / the / the weekend / best … *The best thing about the weekend is …*

2 about / the / thing / is / worst / being my age …

____

3 is / that / thing / one / really / me / annoys / about the media …

____

4 advantage / the / of / being able to / biggest / is/ speak English …

____

5 Complete the sentences in Ex 4 so they are true for you.

Example: *The best thing about the weekend is not having to do any work.*

1 ____________________________

2 ____________________________

3 ____________________________

4 ____________________________

Unit 3

1 Complete the sentences by joining them to the correct feature.

1 He / She really gets up my …

2 He / She never has a … out of place.

3 His / Her antics always raise a few …

4 Success has really gone to his / her …

5 He / She's never out of the public …

6 His / Her name is on everyone's …

2 Match the 'body' idioms in Ex 1 with the definitions.

a always in the press and other media ☐

b made him / her arrogant ☐

c people are talking about him / her ☐

d looks very neat and tidy ☐

e annoys and irritates ☐

f shock, surprise or annoy people ☐

3 Rephrase the sentences replacing the underlined words with an expression that includes the words in *italics*.

Example:
Just show determination and get on with it. *grit / teeth*

Just grit your teeth and get on with it.

1 I'll be wishing you good luck. *keep / fingers*

____

2 You should relax and enjoy yourself once in a while. *let / hair*

____

3 I want to thank you very, very much. *bottom / heart*

____

4 Stop criticising me! *get off / back*

______________________________!

5 It impressed me very much. *blew / mind*

____

4 Complete the mini-dialogues with the *say* or *speak* phrases.

as we were saying I have to say speaking of that said

1 **A:** We're going to see that *Pink Floyd* tribute band next month. Fancy it?

B: Maybe, I'll see. And __________ __________ tribute bands, have you heard Sam's getting a *Coldplay* one together. I think they're calling it *Oldplay* or something.

2 **A:** What do you think of their new album?

B: Not that great, to be honest. __________, it does have a couple of decent tracks on it. And, __________ earlier, their albums do tend to grow on you.

A: Yeah, not their best, but __________ I still quite like it.

as they say don't say I've said it before and I'll say it again let's say personally speaking so to speak

3 **A:** I thought you were a big *Radiohead* fan.

B: Well, like millions, I was. But, __________, when bands start making those awful self-indulgent albums, they deserve exactly what they get if their popularity takes a dive.

4 **A:** I got *The very best of Nashville country* the other day.

B: __________ you're a secret country fan. Surely!

A: Well, variety is the spice of life, __________. And yes, I am a bit of a fan – I can't stand all that commercial 'back home' stuff, __________, but the real, proper country isn't a million miles from, __________, early blues or folk.

B: __________, I'd rather listen to my daughter's TV themes CD.

5 Match words on the left to the terms on the right.

1	URL, P2P, upload	a	football-speak
2	gig, riff, jam	b	music-speak
3	offside, dive, 4-4-2	c	business-speak
4	downsize, turnover, overheads	d	computer-speak

Unit 4

1 Complete the crossword.

Across

5 You give these to pay for something over the phone or the Internet (4, 7)

7 You can *take out*, *pay off* or *default* on this

8 You can have a *current* or *deposit* one of these

9 Deposit = pay _____

10 Another way of saying cash machine

11 You can *deposit*, *transfer* or *withdraw* this

14 This kind of banking means you can make some 1 downs at home

15 This is a record of your recent 1 downs

Down

1 11 across are different kinds of this <u>transaction</u>

2 This is the amount of money you have in, or owe, the bank

3 You can *open*, *close* or *clean out* this (4, 7)

4 This is one of the world's fastest growing crimes (8, 5)

6 You pay this each month when you borrow money

12 Short for Personal Identification Number

13 Withdraw = take _____

2 Put the words in *italics* in the correct order to complete the advice about money matters when travelling abroad.

1 *is / that / recommended / it* ____________________ you keep at least one credit or debit card in the hotel safe at all times and don't ever keep all your money and cards in one place when you are travelling.

2 *not / take / to / care* ____________________ let your credit and debit cards out of your sight.

3 *also / to / want / may / you* ____________________ take some travellers cheques with you.

4 *idea / is / good / it / to / a* ____________________ wear a concealed money-belt when you are out and about.

5 *beware / of / always* ____________________ unofficial money-changers and *sure / always / make* ____________________ you count your money in front of them before you leave.

6 *do, / you / don't / whatever* ____________________ accept damaged notes from anyone – in many countries these are not legal.

3 Choose one or more of the topics in the box and use some of the phrases in Ex 2 to give some good advice.

Example: *When selling something on the Internet, always make sure the payment to you has cleared before you send the item.*

buying or selling things on the Internet studying organising a party attending an interview

1 ____________________

2 ____________________

3 ____________________

4 ____________________

4 Complete these quotes with the correct past form of the verbs in brackets.

1 'In Biblical times, a man (can / have) *could have* as many wives as he (can / afford) ____________________. Just like today.' (Abigail Van Buren, US advice columnist, 1918 –)

2 'The worst thing you can possibly do is worry and think about what you (can / be) ____________________.' (Georg Christoph Lichtenberg, German scientist, 1742–1799)

3 'It's never too late to be who you (might / be) ____________________.' (George Eliot, UK novelist, 1819–1880)

4 'The hardest work in the world is that which (should / do) ____________________ yesterday.' (Anonymous)

5 'It seems to me probable that anyone who has a series of intolerable positions to put up with (must / be) ____________________ responsible for them to some extent.' (Robert Hugh Benson, UK priest and author, 1871–1914)

5 Look at this quote and write a few sentences about your life using *could have, might have* and *should have*.

'Don't fear failure so much that you refuse to try new things. The saddest summary of a life contains three descriptions: could have, might have and should have.' (Louis E. Boone, US Author, 1941–)

Grammar reference

Unit 1

The perfect

Form

You form the perfect simple with an appropriate form of *have* + past participle.

Present perfect simple:
*He's **been** here for hours.*
***Have** you **spoken** to him yet?*
*I **haven't been** there.*

Past perfect simple:
*She **had** just **left**.*

Future perfect simple:
*I'll **have been** here for two years next week.*

You form the perfect continuous with an appropriate form of *have* + *been* + *-ing*.

Present perfect continuous:
*He's **been working** hard.*
***Have** you **been waiting** long?*

Past perfect continuous:
*We'**d been travelling** for days.*

Future perfect continuous:
*We'**ll have been going** out together for exactly a year on Friday.*

Use

You use the perfect to talk about a present, past or future situation that is connected in some way with something that happened or started before it.

This connection could be (1) that there is an important consequence or relevance of a previous action or (2) that the action or situation continues to the time referred to.

But what is important is that the situation at the time referred to is the focus, and details (such as when and how etc) of what happened before it are generally of secondary importance.

She's lost her keys. (She doesn't have her keys now because she lost them.)

We've been waiting for ages. (We're still waiting and we started waiting ages ago.)

I'd been driving all day. (At the end of the day I was tired because I was driving all day.)

She'd already left when we got there. (She wasn't there when we got there because she left earlier.)

The perfect is also sometimes explaiined as being used to express an action in a particular time period that continues to the time referred to.

I've never been to Egypt. (in the period of my lifetime)

I'd never seen anything like it. (in the period up to the time when I saw it)

I'll have had a look at it by then. (in the period between now and 'then')

The simple generally emphasises completion and result and considers the action or situation as a whole.

The continuous generally emphasises continuous or repeated activity and duration.

I've been to New York a couple of times.
I've been going to New York a lot recently.
At last, I've fixed it.
I'd been trying to fix it for about an hour.

Unit 2

Focusing attention

You can focus attention on what you are saying in a variety of ways. One of the most useful ways is to use the following structures.

It is / was ... that / who ...

Whereas in most sentences the new information and / or the information that you want to focus attention on comes at the end, with this structure you put it immediately after *It is / was*.

***It was** David **who** came up with the idea.*
***It is** the precedent that this sets **that** is causing concern.*

What ... is / was ...

With *What … is / was …* the information you want to focus attention on comes at the end.
***What** was different about their idea was that it made use of recycled material.*
***What** gets me is the money they are paid.*

You can use the structure to focus on either the subject or the object of a sentence.
*I don't understand **why he's so popular**.*
*What I don't understand is **why he's so popular**.*
***Her ambition and drive** impresses me.*
*What impresses me is **her ambition and drive**.*

You can also use other question words in this structure.
***How long** you stay **is** up to you.*
***Who** you see **is** none of my business.*

Noun phrase + *is / was ...*

The information you want to emphasise comes at the end. The noun phrase helps introduce it.

***The main problem is** how to accommodate so many people.*
***The key issue is** does it actually work?*

Unit 3

Spoken phrases with *say* and *speak*

English has many spoken phrases that include a form of *say* or *speak*. Here are some of the more common ones.

As they say... (to show it's the opinion of a lot of people)
As they say, if you've got it flaunt it.

I've said it before and I'll say it again, ... (to give emphasis by referring to something previously stated)
I've said it before and I'll say it again, the money that top footballers are paid is a disgrace.

Let's say ... (to give an example)
I can't stand busy pubs. I'd rather go to, let's say, a quiet bar or café or something.

As I was saying ... (to refer back to something you have previously said)
As I was saying, shall we get together sometime next week?

I have to say ... (to emphasise a statement, often when it may seem to contradict something)
It was a long way up, but I have to say, the view from the top was well worth the effort.

That said, ... (to add an opinion that seems to be the opposite of what you have just said, although you think both are true)
It's very expensive. That said, the food is very good.

..., so to speak (to show you have expressed something in an unusual way)
Members of parliament were back in school today, so to speak.

Speaking of ... (to introduce something new that you are going to say relating to a subject that someone has just mentioned)
Speaking of money, have we paid those bills yet?

Unit 4

Using modals to express real and unreal past situations

Real past situations

Modal verbs that express 'real' situations that actually existed or happened change their form:

can → could
will → would
must / have to → had to
I couldn't *phone you – the battery was dead.*
We ***had to*** *wear a uniform at school.*
He said he ***would*** *be there at about 8.30.*

Unreal past situations

The past form of modal verbs that express 'unreal' ideas such as speculation, deduction or hypothesis is:

modal verb + *have* + past participle
Do you think she ***might have left*** *already?*
It ***must have been*** *Sara who told them.*
I couldn't have got *there any earlier.*

Can only expresses real situations. Therefore its past form is *could*, and not *can have* + past participle.

However, *can't* + *have* + past participle is possible, and is used to make a deduction that something is impossible.
~~*She can have worked harder.*~~
She could have worked harder.
She can't have worked harder.

Wordlist

*** the 2,500 most common English words, ** very common words, * fairly common words

Unit 1

a load of rubbish *expr* /ə ˌləʊd əv ˈrʌbɪʃ/
alarmed *adj* /əˈlɑːmd/
alliteration *n* /əˌlɪtəˈreɪʃn/
annoyed *adj* /əˈnɔɪd/ **
astonished *adj* /əˈstɒnɪʃt/ *
badly written *adj* /ˌbædli ˈrɪtn/
behavioural *adj* /bɪˈheɪvjərəl/ *
bicker *v* /ˈbɪkə/
blissfully *adv* /ˈblɪsfəli/
blurt out *v* /ˌblɜːt ˈaʊt/
cajole *v* /kəˈdʒəʊl/
clench *v* /klentʃ/
controversial *adj* /ˌkɒntrəˈvɜːʃl/ **
curse *v* /kɜːs/ *
delve *v* /delv/ *
desperate *adj* /ˈdespərət/ **
dismayed *adj* /dɪsˈmeɪd/
fiddle with *v* /ˈfɪdl wɪð/ *
gesticulate *v* /dʒeˈstɪkjʊˌleɪt/
give sb / sth a wide berth *expr* /ˌgɪv … ə ˌwaɪd ˈbɜːθ/
hesitant *adj* /ˈhezɪtənt/
hilarious *adj* /hɪˈleəriəs/
hopeful *adj* /ˈhəʊpfl/ *
in-depth *adj* /ˈɪn ˌdepθ/
informative *adj* /ɪnˈfɔːmətɪv/ *
inspiring *adj* /ɪnˈspaɪərɪŋ/
interpose (my)self *v* /ˌɪntəˈpəʊz (maɪ)ˌself/
irritation *n* /ˌɪrɪˈteɪʃn/ *
lose count of the number of times *phr* /ˌluːz ˈkaʊnt əv ðə ˌnʌmbər əv ˌtaɪmz/
metaphor *n* /ˈmetəfə, -fɔː/ *
monotonous *adj* /məˈnɒtənəs/
moving *adj* /ˈmuːvɪŋ/ **
mystified *adj* /ˈmɪstɪˌfaɪd/
other half *expr* /ˌʌðə ˈhɑːf/
perplexed *adj* /pəˈplekst/
plead *v* /pliːd/ **
poetic *adj* /pəʊˈetɪk/ *
pound *v* /paʊnd/ *
proportion *n* /prəˈpɔːʃn/ ***
quirk *n* /kwɜːk/
refer to sb / sth as *phr* /rɪˈfɜː tə … əz ˌ…/ ***
simile *n* /ˈsɪməli/
slow-starter *n* /ˌsləʊ ˈstɑːtə/ *
static *n* /ˈstætɪk/
strimmer *n* /ˈstrɪmə/
superficial *adj* /ˌsuːpəˈfɪʃl/ *
tearjerker *n* /ˈtɪəˌdʒɜːkə/
trashy *adj* /ˈtræʃi/
tread on thin ice *expr* /ˌtred ɒn ˌθɪn ˈaɪs/
unmanageable *adj* /ʌnˈmænɪdʒəbl/
unputdownable *adj* /ˌʌnputˈdaʊnəbl/

Unit 2

Are you having me on? *expr* /ə juː ˌhævɪŋ miː ˈɒn/
arouse *v* /əˈraʊz/ **
attribute *n* /ˈætrɪˌbjuːt/ *
blood transfusion *n* /ˈblʌd trænsˌfjuːʒn/
bring it home *expr* /ˌbrɪŋ ɪt ˈhəʊm/
cause concern *phr* /ˌkɔːz kənˈsɜːn/
cell *n* /sel/ ***
come about *v* /ˌkʌm əˈbaʊt/
commodity *n* /kəˈmɒdəti/ **
deep down *adv* /ˌdiːp ˈdaʊn/
die down *v* /ˌdaɪ ˈdaʊn/
donor *n* /ˈdəʊnə/ *
echo *v* /ˈekəʊ/ **
embryo *n* /ˈembriəʊ/
fatal *adj* /ˈfeɪtl/ **
genetic *adj* /dʒəˈnetɪk/ **
get (my) head around sth *expr* /ˌget (maɪ) ˈhed əˌraʊnd/
give rise to *expr* /gɪv ˈraɪz tuː/
inspire sympathy *phr* /ɪnˌspaɪə ˈsɪmpəθi/
intrinsically *adv* /ɪnˈtrɪnsɪkli/
It doesn't matter *expr* /ɪt ˈdʌzənt ˌmætə/
live up to sb's standards *expr* /ˌlɪv ʌp tə … ˈstændədz/
make headlines *phr* /ˌmeɪk ˈhedlaɪnz/
never cease to amaze (me) *phr* /ˌnevə ˌsiːs tuː əˈmeɪz miː/
offspring *n* /ˈɒfsprɪŋ/ *
one thing (I) (really) object to *phr* /ˌwʌn θɪŋ (aɪ) (ˈrɪəli) əbˌdʒekt tuː/
perfectionist *n* /pəˈfekʃnɪst/
play down *v* /ˌpleɪ ˈdaʊn/
rekindle debate *expr* /riːˌkɪndl dɪˈbeɪt/
revolutionary *adj* /ˌrevəˈluːʃnri/ **
rule out *v* /ˌruːl ˈaʊt/
screening *n* /ˈskriːnɪŋ/ *
set a precedent *phr* /ˌset ə ˈpresɪdənt/ *
spell out *v* /ˌspel ˈaʊt/
touch on *v* /ˈtʌtʃ ˌɒn/
Whatever *expr* /wɒtˈevə/
Who cares? *expr* /ˌhuː ˈkeəz/
You're kidding me, aren't you? *expr* /ˌjɔː ˈkɪdɪŋ miː ˌɑːnt juː/

Unit 3

a bunch of *expr* /ə ˈbʌntʃ əv/
a fleeting glimpse *phr* /ə ˌfliːtɪŋ ˈglɪmps/
antics *n pl* /ˈæntɪks/
as I was saying *expr* /ˌæz aɪ wəz ˈseɪɪŋ/
as they say *expr* /əz ˌðeɪ ˈseɪ/
blow (your) mind *expr* /ˌbləʊ (jɔː) ˈmaɪnd/
chuck (your) money about *phr* /ˌtʃʌk (jɔː) ˈmʌni əˌbaʊt/
Come on, let your hair down! *expr* /ˈkʌm ɒn ˌlet jɔː ˈheə daʊn/
couldn't care less *phr* /ˌkʊdnt keə ˈles/
emulate *v* /ˈemjʊˌleɪt/ *
endorse *v* /ɪnˈdɔːs/ **
exploits *n pl* /ˈeksplɔɪts/
freeloader *n* /ˈfriːˌləʊdə/
Get off my back! *expr* /ˌget ɒf maɪ ˈbæk/
glossy *adj* /ˈglɒsi/ *
hang out (your) dirty laundry *expr* /ˌhæŋ aʊt (jɔː) ˌdɜːti ˈlɔːndri/
(success) has gone to (your) head *expr* /(səkˌses) həz ˌgɒn tə (jɔː) ˈhed/
have got more money than sense *expr* /həv ˌgɒt mɔː ˌmʌni ðən ˈsens/
I have to say *expr* /aɪ ˈhæf tə ˌseɪ/
I've said it before and I'll say it again *expr* /ˌaɪv ˈsed ɪt bɪˌfɔː ənd ˌaɪl ˈseɪ ɪt əˌgen/
Keep your eyes open! *phr* /ˌkiːp jɔː ˈaɪz ˌəʊpən/
Keep your fingers crossed! *expr* /ˌkiːp jɔː ˈfɪŋgəz ˌkrɒst/
let's say *expr* /ˈlets ˌseɪ/
never have a hair out of place *expr* /ˌnevə hæv ə ˌheər aʊt əv ˈpleɪs/
nostalgia *n* /nɒˈstældʒə/
on everyone's lips *expr* /ɒn ˌevriwʌnz ˈlɪps/
Personally speaking *phr* /ˈpɜːsnəli ˌspiːkɪŋ/
put (your) heart and soul into sth *expr* /ˌput (jɔː) ˌhɑːt ən ˈsəʊl ɪntə/
raise eyebrows *expr* /ˌreɪz ˈaɪbraʊz/
seventh heaven *expr* /ˌsevnθ ˈhevn/
so to speak *phr* /ˌsəʊ tə ˈspiːk/
so-called *adj* /ˈsəʊ ˌkɔːld/
soul mate *n* /ˈsəʊl ˌmeɪt/
Speaking of *expr* /ˈspiːkɪŋ əv/
star-struck *adj* /ˈstɑː ˌstrʌk/
tabloid *adj* /ˈtæblɔɪd/
thank sb from the bottom of (your) heart *expr* /ˈθæŋk … frəm ðə ˌbɒtəm əv (jɔː) ˈhɑːt/
That said *expr* /ˌðæt ˈsed/
(in / out of) the public eye *expr* /ˌ(ɪn, aʊt) əv ðə ˌpʌblɪk ˈaɪ/
turn heads *expr* /ˌtɜːn ˈhedz/
Use your head! *expr* /juːz jɔː ˈhed/
wait on sb hand and foot *expr* /ˌweɪt ɒn … ˌhænd ən ˈfʊt/
You scratch my back and I'll scratch yours *expr* /juː ˌskrætʃ ˈmaɪ ˌbæk ən ˌaɪl ˌskrætʃ ˈjɔːz/

Unit 4

a complete nightmare *expr* /ə kəmˌpliːt ˈnaɪtmeə/
affiliation *n* /əˌfɪliˈeɪʃn/
bank balance *n* /ˈbæŋk ˌbæləns/
beware of sb (+ -ing) *phr* /bɪˈweər əv …/ *
bill *n* /bɪl/ ***
burst *v* /bɜːst/ **
clean out *v* /ˈkliːn ˌaʊt/
close *v* /kləʊz/ ***
con-artist *n* /ˈkɒn ˌɑːtɪst/
consider (+ -ing) *phr* /kənˈsɪdə/ ***
counterfeit *adj* /ˈkaʊntəfɪt/
criminal record *n* /ˌkrɪmɪnl ˈrekɔːd/
current account *n* /ˌkʌrənt əˈkaʊnt/
default on *v* /dɪˈfɒlt ˌɒn/
deposit *v* /dɪˈpɒzɪt/ **
endanger *v* /ɪnˈdeɪndʒə/
file sharing program *n* /ˈfaɪl ˌʃeərɪŋ ˌprəʊgræm/
financial fraud *n* /faɪˌnænʃl ˈfrɔːd/
get sth (all) sorted out *phr* /ˌget … (ˌɔːl) ˌsɔːtɪd ˈaʊt/
go undetected *phr* /ˌgəʊ ˌʌndɪˈtektɪd/
hack (into) *v* /ˈhæk (ˌɪntə)/ *
high-occupancy *adj* /ˈhaɪ ˌɒkjʊpənsi/
high-ranking *adj* /ˈhaɪ ˌræŋkɪŋ/
I should have thought (that) *phr* /ˌaɪ ˈʃʊd həv ˌθɔːt (ðət)/
I'm convinced (that) *phr* /ˌaɪm kənˈvɪnst (ðət)/
I've come to the conclusion (that) *phr* /ˌaɪv ˈkʌm tə ðə kənˌkluːʒn (ðət)/
I've no doubt at all (that) *phr* /ˌaɪv ˈnəʊ ˌdaʊt ət ˌɔːl (ðət)/
identity theft *n* /aɪˈdentəti ˌθeft/
illegitimate *adj* /ˌɪləˈdʒɪtəmət/
impoverished *adj* /ɪmˈpɒvərɪʃt/
inflatable *adj* /ɪnˈfleɪtəbl/
interest *n* /ˈɪntrəst/ ***
it is recommended (that) *phr* /ˌɪt ɪz rekəˈmendɪd (ðət)/
lane *n* /leɪn/ **
loan *n* /ləʊn/ ***
motive *n* /ˈməʊtɪv/ **
one simple way to prevent sb / sth (+ -ing / being + past part) *phr* /ˈwʌn ˌsɪmpl ˌweɪ tə prɪˌvent/
online banking *n* /ˌɒnlaɪn ˈbæŋkɪŋ/
pass (sb / sth / yourself) (off) as (sb / sth) *expr* /ˌpɑːs … (ˈɒf) əz/
pay off *v* /ˌpeɪ ˈɒf/
phishing *n* /ˈfɪʃɪŋ/
pose as *v* /ˈpəʊz əz/
precaution *n* /prɪˈkɔːʃn/ *
pull off the stunt *expr* /ˈpʊl ɒf ðə ˌstʌnt/
purport *v* /pəˈpɔːt/
safe *n* /seɪf/ *
security *n* /sɪˈkjʊərəti/ ***
spyware *n* /ˈspaɪweə/
take care (not) to (+ inf) *phr* /ˈteɪk ˌkeə (nɒt) tə/
take out *v* /ˌteɪk ˈaʊt/
telemarketer *n* /ˈteliˌmɑːkətə/
transfer *v* /trænsˈfɜː/ ***
valuables *n pl* /ˈvæljʊblz/
(I) wasn't / weren't born yesterday *expr* /(aɪ) ˌwɒznt, ˌwɜːnt ˌbɔːn ˈjestədeɪ/
withdraw *v* /wɪðˈdrɔː/ **

Communication activities

Unit 1, Language study Ex 5 page 36

Top ten annoying habits that can get nasty.

1 Fabricating anecdotes
2 Public use of pet names
3 Taking excessive volumes of luggage on holiday
4 Making your partner spend far longer than they want shopping
5 Laughing at your own jokes when others do not
6 Complaining about or not being interested in your partner's clothes
7 Changing the controls on the car stereo
8 Stealing chips from your partner's plate
9 Spending too long on the computer or playing computer games
10 Leaving clothes lying around

(Based on research by Louisville University, Kentucky)

Unit 2, Lead-in Ex 2 page 38

Dolly the sheep was the first mammal to be cloned. She was cloned from adult cells at a research institute in Scotland in 1996. Dolly later reproduced several offspring of her own through normal means. Scientists claimed cloning animals would allow them to reliably reproduce genetically modified animals for farming purposes and even to provide organs for use in humans. However, it was claimed that Dolly suffered from premature ageing and arthritis, and although many other animals have since been cloned, the process is risky and can lead to deformity. Dolly died in 2003.

Unit 2, Vocabulary and pronunciation Ex 4 page 41

Student A

Look at these conversation openers. Choose one and role-play a conversation with student B. Continue the conversation as long as possible. If the conversation runs out, pick another opener – or think of your own.

a I got a phone call today from somebody I haven't seen for five years.
b I saw your boyfriend / girlfriend kissing somebody else.
c We haven't got any milk.
d Real Madrid have won the Champion's League.

Unit 3, Listening and speaking Ex 7 page 42

Read the rolecard and act out the role-play.

Rolecard

You feel very nostalgic for your childhood and school years. In your room you have lots of momentos and photos that remind you of happy days in the past. You like to watch DVDs of TV programmes and films that you grew up with, and you keep in touch with lots of friends from school, although you have moved to a new city to go to college.

You share a flat with another student who has also moved away from home but is very happy to make a clean break. This evening your flatmate wants to go to a film with you, but you'd rather stay in with your DVDs and your photos.

First make a list of reasons why nostalgia and reminiscing are a good thing. Then answer your flatmate's accusations.

Unit 4, Speaking Ex 1 page 49

Group A

You are members of your town council. You have decided to introduce CCTV cameras in the town centre in an attempt to reduce the high crime rate.

1 First decide how many cameras you need, where you will place the cameras and what result you hope this will have.
2 You are at a meeting with the Town Centre Residents' Association. Role-play the meeting. Start off by presenting your ideas, then listen to and respond to the concerns of the residents.
3 Come to an agreement with the Residents' Association.

Listening scripts

Unit 1 Telling tales

Listening script 13

Reading text from page 35

Listening script 14

He survived the minute only to find that the clock had begun another. And then he knew, with a sense of furious sadness, that this would be followed by another minute, and another, and throughout each one he would be like he was now, only worse.

He wrote to Catherine. *Please come back to me. I want you. I am sober.*

He dropped the letter off in Corrloch and went into O'Malley's bar and bought a bottle of vodka. He walked across the fields with the dog and lay down on the old bed.

The skipper met him on the road as he was setting off for Corrloch.

'Jack,' he said. 'Have you finished with the writing?'

'I think so.'

'Good, I need you out on the blue.'

'When?'

'Tomorrow. We could get in a couple of weeks before the storms. The forecast is good.'

He would have refused but could not. De Largey came for him in a car. They drove down the valley in silence. They went to sea for two weeks after the flatfish. It was a sober, spiritual time.

Listening script 15

He was standing one morning by the skipper in the wheelhouse. On the radio, various voices of other fishermen were cajoling, complaining, cursing, talking of the forthcoming storms. Their voices were always in the background, and sometimes the sound of the radio would drown out the sound of the sea. Then suddenly Jack heard Catherine's voice.

'Calling the *Blue Cormorant*.'

The strange feeling of her personality at the end of the radio unnerved him. Each nuance was hers and yet not hers. She was present in the small engine room in a disembodied way, full of tact, irony, and sounding genteel.

'That's for you, I'll warrant,' said the skipper.

'That's Catherine,' said Jack, disbelievingly.

'Jack,' she said. 'Are you there?'

'Jack Ferris here. Over.'

'When will you be coming in?'

'Friday at eight. Over.'

'Oh, that's a pity. Did you get my letters?'

Jack looked around and whispered into the mike: 'No. Over.'

'That's strange. You should have had them by now.'

'They haven't arrived, Catherine. Over.'

'You don't sound like yourself.'

'Neither do you. Over.'

'Have you been drinking?'

'No,' he lied. 'Over.'

'Well, that's wonderful. You sound very business-like. Over.'

'Under the circumstances, so would you. Over.'

'Am I embarrassing you?'

Her voice, filled with static, cut through the quiet, while the boat drifted in a calm east wind on a sea that was suddenly without landmarks, on a day that could have belonged to any of the seasons, in a sea that could have been any sea.

'I've made my mind up what to do. I'm sure you'll be glad to know.'

'You have? Tell me. Over.'

The radio gave a hoarse crackle. A whistle blew. A sound like a strimmer went through the airwaves.

'What did you say? Can you please repeat the message, Catherine? Over.'

'I'll be down next weekend. I'll leave a letter in the house.'

'See you then. Over.'

'Goodbye, Jack. Over.'

'Goodbye, Catherine. Over.'

He threw open the door of the light-keeper's house. He stepped into the hallway and found the letter for which he had prepared himself waiting inside the hall door. Then his heart began its furious beat. He kissed the damp envelope and tore it open. *It was good to hear your voice. I hope your remember your promise to me. We must stay sober. And I have to admit I'm also fighting off wretched imaginings that someone else will be enjoying you in my place – but I'm trusting you, treading thin ice in the hope that someday we'll be skating along without fear.*

I love you.

His world had been magically restored. The nightmare was over.

Jack, she had written. *I love you and want to be with you. We have a break this weekend and I'll be down to see you. There are other people and we could be with them. But we know we want to be with each other. Let's grow old and sober together.*

He saw himself waiting on the bridge the following afternoon. He saw her alight from the car and begin running towards him. Overcome with happiness he sat there in the December dusk. The bark of a dog flew by.

Unit 2 A perfect world

Listening script 16

Reading text from page 39

Listening script 17

(Z = Zoe, E = Ellie)

Z: What's all that noise? … Ellie, it's 2 o'clock in the morning. Why on earth are you hoovering the living room now?

E: Oh, sorry Zoe. I didn't mean to wake you up. It's just, well, you now my mum's coming tomorrow and I want everything to look tidy.

Z: You're kidding me, aren't you? You're hoovering at 2 o'clock in the morning just because your mum's coming. Who cares if there's a bit of dust?

E: You haven't met my mum yet, have you? She's got a thing about cleaning and everything being tidy. As soon as she gets through the door, she'll look how clean everywhere is. She'll be peering in the fridge and the oven and checking out the bathroom …

Z: Yeah, but so what? I mean we're students, she won't expect everything to be perfect.

E: Well, actually that's where you're wrong. My mum's a perfectionist, she likes everything to be in its proper place and she's really fussy about everything she does. She even irons socks!

Z: Are you having me on? How can you iron socks? … It certainly sounds like she expects a lot from people! But it doesn't mean you have to worry about it. You've left home now, this is your place, not hers.

E: Yeah, I know, it's stupid. Perhaps I'm more like my mum than I imagined. What a horrible thought!

Z: Mm, now I think about it, you are a bit of a perfectionist yourself. I mean, you're totally organised. All your CDs are in alphabetic order and your shoes together in neat rows.

E: OK, OK, I know I'm strange like that. But at least I'm not as bad as my mum. She can't stand other people not living up to her standards and when people do things wrong – well!

Z: Mm. Your mum sounds lovely, I'm really looking forward to meeting her!

E: Oh, she's OK deep down. … Listen, sorry, I woke you. I know you've got to get up early tomorrow.

Z: Oh, it doesn't matter, I'll put the alarm on … see you in the morning.

E: Yeah, 'night. … I think I'll just clean the fridge before I go to bed …

Z: Whatever. Just do it quietly!

Listening script 18

Vocabulary and pronunciation Ex 3 from page 41.

Unit 3 Modern-day icons

Listening script 19

(I = interviewer, S = Shawn)

I: Oh my gosh, Shawn, you know, it's been about a year since we saw each other last and you were on your way to perform in Switzerland. Yeah, I want you to tell me about that experience. Did you know you would be singing for thirty-six thousand screaming fans before you got there?

S: Had no idea. You know, a lot of us were … we didn't even know what to expect, you know what I mean, going to a different country, as they say, you know, there's different cultures and there's different this and there's different that, I think that the strongest thing that we found out is that music is … is a powerful tool. And it's funny how you can go over there and throw this music at kids who are, you know, 12, 14, 18 years old and it just, you know, blew their minds, and it blew our minds because it just goes to show how strong and universal music really is, and you know it's a tool that is very, very, powerful and …

I: And how universal Elvis is …

S: That's … yeah that was my next point. For a man to be away and out of the public eye, so to speak, physically, let's say, but how he still goes on and on and on, and it's funny. We brought that show over there and we were backstage and we'd gotten there and, you know, we were nervous to begin with, so we kinda peeked out at the crowd and boy, I looked out at that crowd and my knees liked to buckle, I just went, woa, wait a minute, it was something to be sought after, something I'll never forget. Hopefully I'll get a chance to go back there. The people in Switzerland are incredible.

I: They love this. You're bringing them closer to the king, it ... really... you were there, if you missed it the first time round, you're getting it the second time around. You know, it's wonderful.

S: I really appreciate that. We really try to work hard and, I've said it before and I'll say it again, he had impact, impact, impact. And again for a guy like that to have an effect on the world, and I mean that, the world. When you go over to Switzerland and, you know, they're singing stuff like *In the Ghetto* back to you and, it's like, man, you know, we're how many thousands of miles away from the States and ... just amazing, amazing. You know, I'm not necessarily saying I'm filling anybody's shoes, because Lord knows I couldn't do that. God puts special individuals on this earth for a certain reason. He put both hands on Elvis, I swear, you know, unbelievable.

I: Well, you're an inspiration to everyone who wants to pay tribute to him, no matter what their capacity.

S: I appreciate that, to everybody out there who feels that way, you know, I'm trying everything to uphold it, you know, an image is a hard thing to keep up.

Listening script 20

1 last
2 chance
3 gosh
4 everybody
5 world
6 work
7 there
8 swear

Listening script 21

Pronunciation Ex 2 from page 43

Unit 4 Safe and sound?

Listening script 22

Reading text from page 47

Listening script 23

(P = presenter, J = Jody, N = Naseem, L = Lily, A = Alvin)

P: Hello and welcome to *Young Britain*. Today we're looking at the question of video surveillance. According to statistics from Liberty, the UK human rights and civil liberties organisation, Britain is monitored by over 4 million CCTV cameras, making us the most-watched nation in the world. The government claims CCTV prevents crime and helps detect criminals after crimes have taken place. However, some people object to constantly being caught on camera. They think it's an infringement of their civil liberties. So, let's hear what you think. Let's take our first caller ... Jody from Sheffield. Hello, Jody.

J: Hello, ...er, well, I just want to say that I definitely support having cameras everywhere. I've felt a lot safer in my area, particularly at night, since we've had cameras ... and er I'm convinced they help stop people from committing crimes. You know, if their faces are gonna be on camera, then people think twice about doing something illegal. There used to be a lot of problems on our estate, you know, like drug dealing and mugging, and now the situation's got a lot better. I don't think that could have happened without CCTV.

P: OK, thanks Jody. And I have to say Jody's opinion does reflect that of the public at large. Most people firmly believe that video surveillance has made them feel safer. ... Right, on to our next caller. And it's Naseem from Birmingham.

N: Hi, ... you know, what I don't understand is why everyone is so positive about these cameras. I mean, it's just harassment, right? ... My mate was charged with a crime he didn't commit when there was a break-in at our local supermarket. The CCTV images were so unclear it could have been anybody. But they marched my mate off to the police station because he's got a police record and said he matched the person on the film.

P: And what happened then?

N: Well, it turned out he was at work when the break-in happened, didn't it? Just like he'd been saying all along. People are supposed to be innocent until proved guilty, aren't they?

P: OK, Naseem, thanks for that. Well, looking at the statistics, there have been a considerable number of misidentifications due to poor-quality images but the technology is improving all the time. Our next caller is Lily from Oxford. Hello Lily.

L: Hello. Well, I should have thought privacy ought to be the main issue here. These cameras are totally in-your-face everywhere you go. You don't know who's watching through these cameras and what they do with the film they take. Remember the case last week? The camera operators were using a camera to spy on a woman in her bathroom, taking pictures of her in the shower. I've come to the conclusion that we can't be expected to have faith in video surveillance, you know, when things like that happen.

P: Well to be quite honest, Lily, how often does something like that happen? I mean, isn't it the case that if you've got nothing to fear, then why let the cameras bother you?

L: Well, I've got nothing to hide, but it's the basic principle, isn't it? Why should we accept people spying on us?

P: OK, Lily let's turn that question over to the next caller and that's Alvin from London. Hello Alvin. How would you answer Lily's question?

A: Well, she's obviously never been in a situation like I have. I was mugged last month in broad daylight, out on the street, you know, on a Saturday afternoon. This guy just hit me in the face and took my mobile. The streets were packed but there no witnesses because there was so much going on and it was all over so quickly.

P: But the crime was caught on camera?

A: That's right. And two weeks later, they got the guy that did it. So I've no doubt at all that we need CCTV.

P: OK, thanks Alvin. We'll take a break now and then be right back. And if you want to call in with your opinion, remember our number is 021 ...

Unit 5 Review

Listening script 24

(B = Ben, A = Anna)

B: ... and I think she's fantastic. All her films have been just brilliant.

A: You know it never ceases to amaze me just how much all these Hollywood stars get paid for a film. I think it's disgusting. I mean, 20 or 30 million dollars for just a few weeks work. It just seems to be getting more and more ridiculous. Don't you think?

B: Well, yes, but the films do earn a vast amount, so as a percentage of the earnings the star's fee is probably not that great. And without a big name, the film wouldn't do nearly as well. That said, I do agree that it's maybe getting a little out of hand. And footballers too, getting, like, £150,000 a week! Now that is crazy.

A: Yeah. And another thing that really annoys me is all the ludicrous things that these stars spend their money on. You know, stuff like gold-plated bathroom taps, million-dollar barbecue sets, bottles of wine that cost thousands, diamond-studded collars for their irritating little pet dogs and so on.

B: Yes, I have to say it can be pretty gross. But as they say, if you've got it, flaunt it.

A: Speaking of 'flaunting it', did you see those hideous pictures the other day of whatshername from that girl band's wedding, you know, the one that's just married that footballer. They got paid a million, or so they say, by some celebrity magazine, just for a few wedding snaps. It's madness. And I read that Elton John actually turned down $6 million to have his wedding televised in the States. But what I don't understand is who on earth is remotely interested enough in all that stuff to warrant the magazines paying such an obscene amount. After all, they're just pictures.

B: I agree, but the right one on the front cover of, let's say, *Hello!* magazine, or something like that, can boost sales massively. I think I remember reading somewhere that the issue with David Beckham's wedding sold three times the normal amount.

A: And the paparazzi – they're just as bad. They've got no real career of their own, so they just make a living out of other people's success. It's the fact that they can get tens of thousands of pounds just for taking dodgy snaps of someone doing their shopping or walking down the street that gets me. And if you ask me, I think the celebrities themselves are behind all this paparazzi stuff a lot of the time. You know, as a way of keeping themselves in the spotlight and on their terms. They might pretend they don't like it, but I wouldn't be surprised if most of the tip-offs come from the celebs themselves.

B: Mm, not sure about that. But as I was saying, I suppose any publicity is good publicity.

A: Well, I suppose so, but what I'd really like to know is who on earth buys these magazines. You always see them in dentists' waiting rooms and such places, but who is actually sad enough to go to the shops to buy a copy?

B: Erm, well ...

A: Don't say you buy them, please. ... Erm, well if you do, you wouldn't happen to have the latest issue of *Hello!* would you? Apparently, there's a really good feature on ....

Listening script 25

Song from page 52

PAIRS

Communication activities

Unit 2, Vocabulary and pronunciation Ex 4 page 41

Student B

Look at these conversation openers. Choose one and role-play a conversation with student A. Continue the conversation as long as possible. If the conversation runs out, pick another opener – or think of your own.

a It's going to rain later.
b I've put on a kilo.
c The TV is broken.
d I'm moving to Argentina.

Unit 3, Listening and speaking Ex 7 page 42

Read the rolecard and act out the role-play.

Rolecard

You are very forward-looking. You prefer to turn your back on the old and get on with the new. As soon as your possessions have outworn practical importance, you throw them away – no point in keeping useless clutter, and you certainly don't keep photo albums.

You are getting increasingly irritated with your flatmate who tends to dwell on the past. This evening you wanted to go to a new film but your flatmate has just said he / she wants to stay in and watch DVDs of old TV series.

First make a list of arguments against nostalgia and living in the past. Role-play the conversation with your flatmate, letting out all your frustration about his / her backward-looking tendencies.

Start like this:

You're not going to watch those old series again? How many times have you seen them now? If I were you ...

Unit 3, Reading and speaking Ex 2 page 45

Quiz score and analysis

Score:

–1 point if you answered 'yes' to questions 4, 6, 9, 15
+1 point if you answered 'yes' to questions 1, 3, 13, 14
+3 points if you answered 'yes' to questions 5, 7, 11, 16
+5 points if you answered 'yes' to questions 2, 8, 10, 12

Analysis:

–4 to 0 You don't give a damn about famous people.

1–10 You find celebrities entertaining, a harmless diversion from dreary everyday reality. This is a harmless level and a healthy emotion.

11–19 Identifying with famous people is natural. But you are overly preoccupied with the lives of the stars and it is probably starting to impinge on your own social life and other interests. Watch out.

20+ You're obsessed with celebrity culture and perhaps overidentify with a single famous person. This could be harmful to your own health – and perhaps to others.

Unit 4, Speaking Ex 1 page 49

Group B

You are the Town Centre Residents' Association for your town. You would like to see crime reduced in your neighbourhood but are sceptical that cameras will achieve this and worried about residents' privacy.

1 First formulate your worries and arguments against cameras.
2 You are at a meeting with members of the council to hear about the CCTV scheme. Listen to the arguments of the council, then ask questions and present your counter-arguments.
3 Come to an agreement with the town council.

Module 3
Groups

Unit	Topic	Language study	Vocabulary	Main skills
1 **Living together** pages 66–69	• Happy families (Britain's biggest family) • A social experiment (living in an alternative community)	• Ellipsis and substitution	• Family relationships • Community organisation	• **Reading:** understanding gist; understanding vocabulary in context • **Speaking:** discussing cultural values and family relationships; discussing the aims of non-traditional living communities • **Listening:** identifying key information • **Writing:** an online advert
2 **Talk talk** pages 70–73	• World languages (Are fewer languages better?) • Language learning (attitudes to learning English and other foreign languages)	• Forming adjectives from verbs and nouns (adjective suffixes)	• Sensitive language (euphemisms)	• **Reading:** predicting; understanding main information and vocabulary in context • **Speaking:** evaluating the cultural and practical value of languages; using sensitive language and softeners to avoid offence • **Listening:** identifying key information • **Pronunciation:** sentence stress
3 **Net value** pages 74–77	• Is the Internet a good thing? • Are you addicted to email? (survey report)	• Using vague language	• Phrasal verbs: communication • Surveys	• **Listening:** understanding gist and key information; understanding vocabulary in context • **Speaking:** discussing the Internet; clarifying information and checking understanding; talking about email addiction; conducting a survey • **Pronunciation:** stress and weak forms • **Reading:** understanding key information • **Writing:** a survey report
4 **Team spirit** pages 78–81	• Team building • Are you a team player?	• Dependent prepositions	• World of work	• **Reading:** predicting information; checking key information and vocabulary in context • **Speaking:** discussing work practices and leadership styles; describing college- or work-related problems and giving advice • **Listening:** identifying key information; understanding vocabulary in context • **Writing:** a programme script

• **Use CD2 for listening activities in this module.**

1 Living together

LEARNING AIMS

- Can use ellipsis and substitution
- Can discuss cultural values and family relationships
- Can discuss the aims of non-traditional living communities

Lead-in

1 Discuss these questions with your class.

1 What do you associate with the word 'family'? Brainstorm ideas.
2 What different types of 'family' are there?
3 Is it possible to be a 'family' without having children?

Happy families

Reading and vocabulary

1 Work with a partner and discuss these questions.

1 What do you think the fertility rate (the average number of births per woman) is in your country? Is there a tendency to having more or fewer children?
2 Do you think small or large families are the norm in Britain? Compare your ideas with the fertility rate on page 93.

2 **01** Read the article on page 67. Answer these questions.

1 How do Sue and Ian Povey feel about having so many children?
2 How do they feel about having even more children?
3 How do their daughters Becky and Charlotte feel about having children?

3 Find the following sentences in paragraphs 4 and 6 of the article and discuss the meaning of the expressions in **bold**.

1 We're very **close**.
2 All the children **muck in**.
3 We both **devote our lives to** the children.
4 As soon as he walks through the door he is **hands on**.
5 He **suffers in silence**.
6 If anybody is **out of line**, she doesn't need to **lose her temper** – she just **gives them a look**.

4 Work with a partner. Which of the words and phrases in Ex 3 have very positive / positive / rather negative / very negative meanings? Make lists.

5 Add these words and phrases to your lists. Use a dictionary to help you.

1 he really **resents** his little brother
2 they never stop **squabbling**
3 she has **the patience of a saint**
4 they **get on like a house on fire**
5 he **neglects** his children
6 she's always **nagging** us
7 we **stick up for** each other
8 there's a lot of **give and take**

6 Work with a partner. Talk about your family or a family you know well.

1. Are you a close family?
2. As children did you have to muck in and help out? In what ways?
3. Was your father a hands-on parent or more of an authority figure?
4. What did your parents do when you were out of line?
5. Do you ever lose your temper in family situations? When?

Britain's biggest brood

SUPERMUM Sue Povey smiled after giving birth to her 15th baby and said: 'I'm not finished yet – I'm already looking forward to sweet sixteen.' Sue, 43, was speaking after taking baby Isabelle home from hospital. She said: 'I just feel so happy and elated. I think having babies keeps me young. It's like a drug. I'm a babyaholic. I definitely want another one – I knew that in my heart the moment the midwife gave me Isabelle to hold.'

Since Sue first gave birth 23 years ago she has never gone more than two years and three months without doing so. She and husband Ian, 45, now have nine girls and six boys. The couple celebrate their 25th wedding anniversary later this year and live with 13 of their children.

Ian, a systems analyst, said, 'Sue said she wanted six children soon after we were married. I thought she was being a bit ambitious and put it down to wishful thinking. We started off with a six-a-side team, then a football 11 and now we have a rugby 15. But I'm really pleased. Even after having 15 children you still experience the same strength of feeling – a new birth is always exciting. The children were thrilled. They all wanted to be the first to see Isabelle and hold her. If nature has its way I'm sure Sue will have another baby. When you've had 15 I don't think another one makes much difference.'

The former hairdresser was determined that her children should have lots of brothers and sisters, simply because she herself didn't. She felt lonely as a child with just one sister, Barbara, who is 13 years older. Sue said, 'I hated being on my own all the time. I was very shy and couldn't make friends easily. I didn't want my children to feel like that. Some people don't approve of large families but I will never change my mind. We're very close. All the children muck in and help each other out. We both devote our lives to the children so they're never short of love. Ian works all day but as soon as he walks through the door he is hands on. He suffers in silence. He's a saint, as well as being a great taxi driver.'

Sue had wanted to have another baby but had almost given up hope of being able to when doctors confirmed she was expecting Isabelle. Sue said, 'I was beginning to feel my biological clock had run out of batteries. It will be absolutely awful when I can no longer have babies. It will feel like a bereavement – like part of me has died. Twins would be the icing on the cake. There's still time.'

Eldest daughter Becky, 22, said, 'Isabelle's beautiful. I'm getting broody. Fair play to mum. She's incredible.' Hairdresser Charlotte, 19, said, 'Originally I said I wasn't going to have any children but now I think I'd like two. But I'm nowhere near as patient as mum. If anybody is out of line she doesn't need to lose her temper – she just gives them a look.'

Speaking **1** Discuss these questions in groups. Then compare your opinions with another group.

1. How do people feel about large families in your country?
2. Why are women in most European countries having fewer children? What are the demographic consequences of this?
3. How should governments encourage families to have more children?
4. Read the text in the panel. What do you think are the advantages and disadvantages of very young and very old mothers? (Consider medical, economic, social and cultural factors.)

> In some countries it is usual and preferable to have children at an early age. In other countries such as the UK, there is a high rate of unwanted teenage pregnancies and many women put off having children until their thirties or forties. Due to scientific advances it is now also possible to have children past the usual childbearing age. For example, a 66-year-old Romanian woman gave birth to a child.

LANGUAGE STUDY

Ellipsis and substitution

1 Ellipsis (omitting words and phrases) and substitution (replacing words and phrases) are two ways of avoiding repeating what has been said. Which of these extracts from the text on page 67 contain examples of:

a ellipsis ☐ ☐ b substitution ☐

1 *Since Sue first gave birth 23 years ago she has never gone more than two years and three months without* ***doing so****.*

2 *The former hairdresser was determined that her children should have lots of brothers and sisters, simply because she herself* ***didn't****.*

3 *Sue had wanted to have another baby but had almost given up hope of* ***being able to*** *when doctors confirmed she was expecting Isabelle.*

2 What has been omitted or substituted in each of the extracts?

Grammar reference page 90

3 Complete these findings from a recent UK survey on marriage and the family with the verbs and phrases in the box.

are doing so	do	not to	to do so	were

1 Despite having taken marriage vows that they will remain together for life, over a third of newly-married couples do not think it is realistic ______________.

2 Almost a fifth of women say they expect to be less involved in raising their children than their mothers ______________.

3 Fewer people are getting married for religious reasons, but ______________ as a way of demonstrating commitment, stability and security.

4 Compared to previous generations there is less pressure to get married in your 20s, and as a result many of today's young adults are choosing ______________.

5 Mothers who don't work while their children are growing up tend to get on better with their children later in life than mothers who ______________.

4 Do you think the findings in Ex 3 would be similar in your country?

5 Read the text and explain what information has been omitted or substituted.
Example: (1) *take time out to go travelling* is omitted.

Home Search Shop Bookmarks

Attitudes to marriage and family – Dave and Jen

Dave Jones and Jen Anderson, both 24-year-old accountants, met in their first year at University. Dave says, 'After university, a lot of our friends took a gap year or two to go travelling, but we decided not to (1). We got jobs and bought a house as soon as we were able to (2), which has doubled in value in just two years. Friends who didn't get on the property ladder when we did (3) are now finding it much more expensive to do so (4). Some of them who did take time out are now wishing they hadn't (5) and I think they're beginning to regret their 'don't be so sensible, life's for living' attitude.

But, on the other hand, I do sometimes wonder if we should've seen a bit more of the world and (6) been a bit more adventurous while we had the chance (7). We might be a bit more tied down than some of our friends and perhaps (8) not have as much freedom and spontaneity as they do (9), but at the same time we've got what they want. Have we made the right choices? I think so (10). We do plan to marry and have kids, but we don't want to do so (11) just yet. We'd like to wait until we are in our 30s. At 24, I'd still rather be buying DVDs than (12) children's shoes.'

6 How is your attitude similar to or different from Dave and Jen's?

A social experiment

Listening and speaking

1 Some people choose not to live in 'mainstream' society and instead choose to live in alternative communities such as communes or housing cooperatives. Why do you think some people make this choice?

2 **02** Listen to a report on Christiania, an alternative living community in Copenhagen. As you listen, tick the things that form a part of Christiania's way of life.

art ☐ common childcare and healthcare ☐ common mealtimes ☐

common ownership of property ☐ democracy ☐ eco-friendly practices ☐

independence from Danish laws ☐ no cars ☐ no electricity or running water ☐

prayer and meditation ☐ unconventional housing ☐

3 Work with a partner and discuss these questions.

1 Opponents of Christiania see the community as 'a scourge on the city'. Why?
2 What problem was Christiania facing at the time of the report?
3 According to the report, nearly a million tourists a year visit Christiania? Why do you think so many people are interested in this alternative community?
4 The report asks the question: *Lawless, elitist and dirty? Or progressive, inventive and free?* What do you think?

Vocabulary

1 Listen to the report again and complete these sentences. Then check your answers in the listening script on page 94.

1 A motley group of hippies, artists and misfits have founded a home that **shuns** ______________, ______________ and ______________.
2 Christiania has been **conducting** ______________ for more than thirty years.
3 They have even **established** ______________.
4 A group of drug-smoking criminals **trespassing** ______________ and **ignoring** ______________ the rest of Denmark have to obey.
5 Liberal governments in the past **adopted** ______________.
6 Residents will have to **register** ______________.
7 The plan seeks to **preserve** ______________________________.
8 All the things that have made the area so special are rooted in the unique way they **administer** ______________ and **prohibit** the ______________________________.

2 Work in a group. Imagine you are setting up your own alternative community. First brainstorm ideas you will establish:

Think about:
1 where you will establish your community and the type of housing;
2 how many people and the sort of people you want to attract;
3 your main principles (rules, prohibitions);
4 whether your community will be self-supporting or have outside financial help?

3 Write an online advert to recruit people for your community, using your ideas in Ex 1 and 2. Start like this: *We are a group of … planning to establish … . We are seeking …*

4 Read the adverts of the other groups. Comment on whether you would be attracted to their community or not, explaining your reasons.

CD-ROM For more activities go to **Groups Unit 1**

2 Talk talk

LEARNING AIMS

- Can form adjectives from verbs and nouns using suffixes
- Can evaluate the cultural and practical value of languages
- Can use sensitive language and softeners to avoid offence

World languages

Lead-in

1 Work with a partner and talk about your first language. Discuss these questions:

1 Where is your first language spoken?
2 What do you know about the history and development of your language?
3 Is there a big difference between the written and spoken forms of your language?
4 How easy or difficult is it for foreign students to learn your language?

Reading and speaking

1 How many languages are spoken in the world today? Agree on an approximate figure as a class. Then read the first two paragraphs of the article on page 71 and find out.

2 03 Read the article in full. Match these summaries to the correct paragraphs.

a Speaking a majority language is considered desirable by many people.
b Documenting endangered languages is the best way to deal with them.
c The number of languages spoken in a country is linked to its degree of isolation.
d The end of a life means the end of a language.
e There has been a significant change in the ratio of the world's population and the number of languages spoken, aided by communication technology.
f People who want to preserve languages seem unaware of the needs of their speakers in the modern world.
g The fact that many of the world's languages are dying is of immense concern.

3 Make a list of minority languages that you know are being used less than in the past. Where are they spoken? In what way has their usage changed?

4 Discuss these issues with the class.

1 What do you think are the advantages of reviving a minority language? Think about issues such as culture, tourism, business, and intellectual gain.
2 What are the problems associated with reviving a minority language? Think about organisation, finance, speakers' way of life, and national unity.
3 On balance, do you agree with the author of the article that saving dying languages isn't actually worth all the effort?

Vocabulary

1 Look at the underlined phrases in these sentences from the article. How would we usually express these sentences more directly? Why do we use euphemisms like these?

When Marie Smith-Jones passes away …
It's only a matter of time before their current speakers fall silent.

2 Work with a partner. Rewrite these euphemisms in more direct language.
Example: Her company had to let her go. *Her company fired her.*

1 He's getting on a bit.
2 She's very careful with money.
3 His shoes have seen better days.
4 I need to go to the bathroom.
5 She's on the large side.
6 They're on a low income.
7 She's between jobs right now.
8 He likes a tipple.

3 Match the words in Box A with the euphemisms in box B.

A	bald dishonest lazy short stupid

B	morally different motivationally deficient mentally challenged hair disadvantaged vertically challenged

4 What other euphemisms have you heard in English / your own language?

Example: *In English people say 'senior citizens' instead of 'old people'. In my language we say 'people in the third age' for old people.*

Are fewer languages better?

1 When Marie Smith-Jones passes away, she will take with her a small but irreplaceable piece of human culture. That's because the octogenarian from Anchorage is the last speaker of Eyak, the traditional language of her Alaskan people.

2 To Unesco – the United Nations Educational, Scientific and Cultural Organisation – language extinction is a disaster of, well, unspeakable proportions. It warns of a 'catastrophic reduction in the number of languages spoken in the world' and estimates 3,000 are 'endangered, seriously endangered, or dying.' In other words, children have stopped learning half the world's languages, and it's only a matter of time before their current speakers fall silent. Unesco calls this an 'irretrievable and tragic' development because 'language diversity' is 'one of humanity's most precious commodities.'

3 But is it really? A growing number of people are speaking a smaller number of languages, meaning that age-old obstacles to communication are collapsing. Surely this is a good thing. Michael Krauss of the University of Alaska believes that 10,000 years ago there may have been as many as 20,000 languages spoken by a total human population of perhaps 10 million. Assuming this is true, it would suggest a connection between more people and fewer languages, and between language and the technology that lets people communicate over distance.

4 That makes sense, because geographic isolation promotes linguistic diversity. A language doesn't require more than a few hundred people to sustain it, assuming they keep to themselves. Papua New Guinea is home to the highest concentration of languages anywhere – at least 820 different tongues. Unesco's report describes Papua New Guinea as 'a fitting example for other civilisations to follow.'

5 That's an odd thing to say about a country where a sizeable proportion of the population doesn't own a phone, but it's typical of the language preservationists, who apparently would like to see tribal members live in primitive bliss, preserving their exotic customs. David Crystal makes the point unwittingly in his book *Language Death* when he describes an Australian aboriginal language 'whose vocabulary provides different names for grubs (an important food source) according to the types of bush where they're found.' He's trying to say that we may become more knowledgeable about biology if we preserve and study obscure languages – but he seems oblivious to the reality that most people would rather eat a Big Mac than a fistful of beetle larvae.

6 The most important reason some languages are disappearing is precisely that their native speakers don't regard them as quite so precious. They view linguistic adaptation as a key to getting ahead. This is understandable when about half the world's population speaks one of only 10 languages and when speaking English in particular is a profitable skill.

7 Each language captures something about a way of life, and when one goes mute, it is hard not to feel a sense of loss. But maybe linguists should try to learn as much as they can about 'dying' languages before they vanish completely, rather than engage in an impracticable attempt to save them.

LANGUAGE STUDY

Forming adjectives from verbs and nouns (adjective suffixes)

1 Look at these extracts from the text on page 71. Match the examples of the suffix *-able* with the uses.

a with verbs to make adjectives describing something that can or can't be done. ☐ ☐ ☐ ☐

b with nouns to make adjectives describing a quality that something has. ☐ ☐

1 *When Marie Smith-Jones passes away, she will take with her a small but* ***irreplaceable*** *piece of human culture.*
2 *Language extinction is a disaster of, well,* ***unspeakable*** *proportions.*
3 *Unesco calls this an* ***'irretrievable*** *and tragic' development.*
4 *A* ***sizeable*** *proportion of the population doesn't own a phone.*
5 *We may become more* ***knowledgeable*** *about biology if we preserve and study obscure languages.*
6 *This is* ***understandable*** *when about half the world's population speaks one of only 10 languages.*

2 Which negative prefixes are used with the adjectives in the extracts? What other common negative prefixes can you use with adjectives?

Grammar reference page 90

3 Complete these sentences with an adjective ending in *-able* formed from the words in the box. You may need to use a negative prefix or change the spelling.

Example: Today, exposure to the English language is largely *unavoidable*.

advise	appreciate	~~avoid~~	download	escape	reputation	size	value

1 It is an ___________ fact, that English has become *the* language to learn.
2 English-speaking personnel are absolutely ___________ for companies doing business in the UK and US as a ___________ proportion of the population of these countries speaks no second language at all.
3 When travelling abroad on business, any attempt to speak in your host's language should make an ___________ difference to any business relationship.
4 When choosing where to study, it is ___________ to make sure the school is ___________ and the teachers have recognised qualifications.
5 Another very useful way of learning a language is via the Internet, which may offer a self-study programme via ___________ lessons.

4 Rephrase these sentences using an adjective ending in *-able* formed from the verb.

Example: You can't describe it. *It's indescribable.*

1 No-one could have stopped it.
2 It can be justified in some cases.
3 It can't be cured.
4 It can't be replaced.
5 It's difficult, but you can do it.
6 It can't be explained.

5 Work with a partner. Think of people and things that can be described by the adjectives in Ex 4.

6 You can also add other suffixes to nouns to form adjectives describing a quality that something or someone has. Copy the table and add each group of words to the appropriate column according to which suffix they take.

1 colour / care / meaning / use / thought / harm
2 child / snob / slug / sheep / style / fool
3 rock / dust / mist / rain / salt / room / mood / hair
4 adventure / danger / fame / number / advantage

-able	*-y*	*-ful*	*-ish*	*-ous*
sizeable				
reputable				
knowledgeable				

7 Work with a partner and add more adjectives to each group in the table. Share your ideas with the class.

The reading material for the subject I want to study is published mainly in English so I can't get round learning the language.

I'd like to improve my employment potential.

Language learning

Listening

1 What is your motivation to learn English?

2 **04** Listen to three students talking about learning English and the role of English in the world. Make notes on:

- their motivation for learning English
- their attitude to English as a *lingua franca*

NOTE

lingua franca
a language people use to communicate when they have different first languages

▲ Tatyana

▲ Lars

▲ Paolo

3 Who do you agree with most? Why?

Speaking and pronunciation

1 The three speakers express strong opinions but they use particular expressions to soften those opinions in order to be polite. Listen again and complete the notes with their 'softeners'.

Tatyana: I ________________ some people don't like that, but ________________, I ________________ think it's unavoidable.

________________ all countries should teach children English when they are small, so they find it easy to learn.

Lars: ________________ I think it's sad that English has become a *lingua franca* and that other languages, you know, are dying out because English is getting more important. ________________, it's practical to have one language you can speak wherever you go.

________________ that English doesn't belong to certain countries anymore. It's just everybody's world language.

Paolo: I've got ________________ a problem with English as a *lingua franca*. I know English is important, ________________ you can't get by without it nowadays, but I ________________ think it would be better if everybody learnt more foreign languages.

But they're ________________ imposing their way of life and their view of the world on other people through their language and a lot of people oppose that.

2 Check the sentences in listening script 04 on page 94. Then listen and read the sentences. Mark the sentence stress in the script by underlining the stressed words. Which of the softeners are stressed in these sentences?

3 Work with a partner. Student A look at page 93. Student B look at page 96.

CD-ROM For more activities go to **Groups Unit 2**

3 Net value

LEARNING AIMS

- Can use vague language in informal communication
- Can evaluate the importance and dangers of electronic media
- Can clarify information and check understanding

Lead-in

1 Work with a partner and talk about the way you use the Internet.

1. How often do you use the Internet for communication with other people (email, chat rooms, internet telephoning, blogging)? How much do you use the Internet on your own (for example, for research, surfing, downloading podcasts)?
2. How much spam* do you get? How much of it do you actually read?
3. What precautions do your take to protect your computer from viruses, spyware and other downloadable threats? What tips do you have for other users?
4. How helpful are your search results when you use a search engine?

*spam = unwanted emails sent to large numbers of people

Is the Internet a good thing?

Listening and speaking

1 Look at the photos from two adverts about the Internet. What aspects of the Internet do they represent?

2 05 Listen to the two adverts and check your ideas in Ex1.

Is the Internet a **good thing**?

Is the Internet a **bad thing**?

3 Listen again. What other good and bad aspects of the Internet do the adverts mention?

4 The adverts ask *What do you think?* Debate this question in your class.

Divide into two groups. Group A: you think the Internet is a good thing. Group B: you think the Internet is a bad thing.

- In your group, think of more arguments for your debate.
- Hold the debate in class.
- Vote to decide which opinion your class agrees with.

Listening and vocabulary

1 **06** Listen to Graham and Layla talking about the internet adverts. Summarise their views about the Internet.

2 Work with a partner. Answer these questions.

1 What does Layla think about the way the adverts get their message across?
2 Why couldn't Graham figure out the adverts at first?
3 What aspects of searching for information on the Internet does Graham point out?
4 According to Layla what does using the Internet boil down to?
5 What is Layla getting at when she summarises her view of the Internet?
6 What was Graham on about when he referred to the information society?

3 Listen again and check your answers in Ex 2.

4 Match the underlined verbs in Ex 2 with the verbs in the box. What is the difference in style between the verbs in Ex 2 and these verbs?

amount to	convey	focus on	talking about	trying to say	understand

5 Complete the sentences. Then read your sentences to a partner and comment on his / her statements.

1 I think that being successful in today's world boils down to …
2 People today are always on about …
3 What nobody has pointed out about the Internet is that …
4 What I can't figure out about computers is …
5 Getting at the truth …
6 I sometimes find it difficult to get across …

Speaking and pronunciation

1 Look at these phrases from the listening text, used to clarify or check understanding. Copy the table and put the phrases in the correct column.

~~What do you mean by …?~~ In other words, you … Do you know what I mean?
What I'm getting at is … Are you with me? What I mean is, …

Speaker clarification	Speaker checking	Listener checking
		What do you mean by ...?

2 Add these phrases to the table in Ex 1.

So what you're trying to say is …	I suppose I'm really saying …
Do you follow?	Do you get me?
If I've understood you correctly …	To put it a different way …

3 **07** Listen to the phrases and check your answers. Then listen again and repeat. Pay attention to weak forms and stress.

4 Discuss aspects of computer and internet technology.

- Note down an opinion about three of the things in the box.
- Work with a partner. Take it in turns to give your opinion, clarifying things if necessary using the appropriate phrases in Ex 1 and 2.
- Respond to your partner's opinion, checking that you have understood by using the appropriate phrases in Ex 1 and 2.

blogging chat rooms internet dating live webcams music file sharing
reliability of computer software and hardware
the rapid pace of computer technology Wikipedia and other wikis

LANGUAGE STUDY

Using vague language

1 Look at these extracts from Listening Ex 1 on page 75. What is the function of the language in **bold**?

1. *All that information* ***and stuff*** *– and it's free!*
2. *I can't imagine not having the Internet for downloading music, shopping* ***and whatever****.*
3. *Well, what about credit card fraud and identity theft* ***and that sort of thing****?*
4. *I think I read that 75%* ***or so*** *of websites are in English.*
5. *Not true. It's 50%, or 50****ish*** *anyway.*
6. *I think the Internet actually helps countries with few resources because it gives them, you know,* ***a kind of*** *platform to make their problems known.*
7. *Yeah, that's the rose-tinted view, the Internet strengthens social bonds* ***and all that****.*

Grammar reference page 91

2 Complete these statements about the Internet by putting the words and phrases in *italics* in an appropriate position.

Example: The computer screen has become a kind of window into a world where reality and unreality are getting more and more confused. *kind of*

1. I really do wonder about privacy on the Internet. When you're chatting or sending emails, how anonymous actually are you? *or whatever*
2. The danger of the Net is that you can become trapped in a vicious cycle of webpages based on webpages with reliable information becoming more and more difficult to find. *kind of*
3. Sites such as ebay are just fantastic. I get stuff from them all the time. *and the like*
4. I just love getting all those email funnies, you know, jokes, quizzes, funny pictures. *and that sort of thing*
5. It's just the best thing ever – information, people, gaming, music, shopping, and all without having to leave the room. *and so on*
6. The best thing is P2P. It's made the Net a global music collection – you think of a song and two minutes later it's on your hard drive, or MP3 player. And it doesn't cost you a cent. *sort of* *or however long* *or whatever*

3 Complete these sentences using an appropriate question word combined with the suffix *-ever*.

Example: I just love going out – pubs, clubs, bars, *wherever*.

1. I'll happily listen to anything – rock, pop, classical, country, opera, ____________.
2. I'd love to have the chance to live abroad – the UK, USA, Japan, ____________.
3. I don't care who wins the cup – Chelsea, Barcelona, AC Milan, ____________.
4. I'm always up for going for a drink – afternoon, early evening, ____________.
5. I'm happy studying anything in English lessons – grammar, vocabulary, reading, ____________.

4 Are any of the sentences in Ex 3 true for you?

5 Work in groups. Ask and answer questions beginning with *How much / How many …? How long …? How far …?* etc and answer them using the phrases in the box.

Example:
A: *How many CDs have you got?* **B:** *I'd say about 100 give or take.*

about	around	getting on for	give or take	-ish	in the region of
more or less	or so	or thereabouts			

Reading and vocabulary

1 Look at the title of the article. What's your answer?

Are you addicted to email?

U.S. residents are so hooked on email that some check for messages in the bathroom, in church, and while driving, a survey sponsored by America Online has found. The average email user in the U.S. has (1) ______ email accounts and spends approximately (2) ______ a day reading, sending, and replying to messages, according to the survey, conducted by Opinion Research.

Email dependency is so strong for (3) ______ of survey respondents that they check their email inbox right after getting out of bed in the morning. The average user checks their inbox (4) ______ times per day, according to the survey.

(5) ______ of respondents acknowledged being so emailaholic that they can't go more than two or three days without checking for messages. That includes vacations, during which (6) ______ of respondents admitted logging in to their inbox.

Unsurprisingly, all that email activity sometimes leads to regrets. (7) ______ of the respondents indicated they would like to have the ability to retrieve a message they have sent but that hasn't been read yet.

There is as well, it seems, some attachment anxiety to sent messages. (8) ______ favoured being able to track where their messages get forwarded.

2 Work with a partner. Read the article and predict what statistics were in spaces 1–8.

3 **08** Check your answers for Ex 2 on page 96. What findings surprised you the most?

4 Look at the language used in the answers to Ex 2. What other phrases do you know for referring to statistics in a survey? Examples: *1 in 10* *just over …*

5 Explain the meaning of these words and phrases from the article.

1 hooked on 2 conducted 3 average 4 respondents 5 retrieve 6 track

6 Work with a partner and discuss these questions.

1 What are you hooked on?
2 Looking at the information in the article, would you say you are an 'average' internet user?
3 How do you usually react when asked to be a respondent in a survey being conducted online or in the street?
4 What are the benefits of being able to retrieve and track email messages?

Speaking and writing

1 Work in groups and conduct your own survey about addiction. First choose one of these questions or think of your own question. Are you addicted to …

… your computer? … text messaging? … your MP3 player?
… shopping? … computer games?

2 In your group, formulate your survey questions.

3 Each person in the group interviews two or three people and notes down their answers.

4 Pool your findings and write a group survey report. Use the phrases in Reading and vocabulary Ex 4 to help you, and words to express the opinions of respondents such as *approved of, agreed with.*

5 Read your report to the class. Which survey had the most interesting findings?

CD-ROM For more activities go to **Groups Unit 3**

4 Team spirit

LEARNING AIMS

- Can use dependent prepositions
- Can discuss work practices and leadership styles
- Can describe college or work-related problems and give advice to others

Lead-in

1 What jobs can you think of where you usually work in a team? In what jobs do you often work alone? Do you prefer working in a team or working alone? Why?

Team building

Reading

1 Look at the activities in the photos on page 79. What are the people doing? Why do you think companies pay a lot of money for employees to do things like this?

2 **09** Read the article on page 79. Work with a partner and decide if the statements are true or false. Find evidence in the text to support your answers.

1. Working in a team often means working with people you wouldn't normally socialise with.
2. Team-building events usually take place at regular intervals throughout the year.
3. The most important goal of team-building events is to have a fun day out.
4. Employees should take an active part in team events.
5. It's beneficial if employees have no expectations of team events.
6. Companies usually stick to tried and tested types of activities.
7. Companies like E3 pay for the cost of team trips.
8. The effects of team-building trips are usually short-lived.

Vocabulary and speaking

1 Work with a partner. Find these phrases in the text and work out their meaning.

1. **face up to** the challenge
2. **utilise** skills
3. go in **with an open mind**
4. **participate** in tasks
5. **tackle** problems
6. **enhance** performance
7. learn to **delegate**
8. **bond** as a team

2 Put an appropriate form of the words or phrases in Ex 1 in these sentences.

1. I was determined to enjoy my new job and went in on the first day ____________ .
2. I ____________ really well with the other people in the office right from the start.
3. I've ____________ in lots of social events with my colleagues outside work.
4. I try to ____________ my experience from holiday jobs as much as possible.
5. I focus on things I find hard and then make an effort to ____________ them.
6. As I'm the most junior office member everybody ____________ the most menial jobs to me.
7. I've ____________ the fact that I'll be making the coffee for a while!
8. The whole experience of starting work has ____________ my life in lots of ways.

Why delegate? I can do everything faster and better myself.

I think participating in a team-building event would be great fun.

Bonding with work colleagues isn't necessary – competition among colleagues is a good thing.

The sort of skills you acquire while tackling problems like learning the drums are not really ones you can utilise later in your work.

3 Rate the statements in the speech bubbles: 5 for strongly agree to 1 for strongly disagree. Then explain and discuss your ratings with a partner.

4 Discuss these questions with your class.

1. Are team-building courses common in your country?
2. Is it usual to socialise with colleagues or other students outside work / study?
3. Do companies or colleges have other ways of creating team spirit in your country?

Get together

Getting up close and personal with a bunch of folks you may never be seen dead with outside work might not be what you bargained for in your career, but it's something you will probably find yourself doing – and possibly enjoying. Many employers see the annual team-building event as the makings of a tight ship in their organisation.

Normally aiming for an eclectic mixture of fun, focus and forward-vision, team awaydays are intended to be more than splattering your colleagues in paint and listening to management-speak, which has little impact on your role once back in the workplace. But can you really expect to gain more from the event than some embarrassing memories?

Well, yes, according to David Evans, chief executive of a company which specialises in improving the performance of other organisations. He feels the image of such events as an excuse for having a knees-up is outdated. 'To be frank we just don't see it today,' says Evans. 'An element of socialising and having fun is part of it, but the management team has to show a return on the investment.'

It is the employee's responsibility, of course, to contribute proactively and face up to the challenge. Caroline Barber recently completed her company's graduate management development programme. She suggests leaving your preconceptions at the door before embarking on any team event. 'Think about what you want to take back into the workplace and how you will utilise the skills learned. Go in with an open mind.'

Team-building days are great for those interested in trying something new. One of the many tasks Barber participated in was a tandem biking exercise around a forest, designed to enhance performance and expose new employees to other people across the business.

And if paint-balling is your preconceived notion of what team-building events are all about, forget it. Employees can anticipate increasingly innovative programmes which force them to tackle unusual problems. Lizzie Barrett is an accounts executive. African drumming was one activity she enjoyed with her team, but not the only one. She says, 'We did circus training last year, which meant we had to learn literally how to juggle, as well as spin plates. It made us aware of timing, control, and ultimately how to delegate, and say no!'

Digital media agency E3 is going a few hundred thousand steps further, taking its entire workforce of 30 on an all-expenses trip to Dubai. Joint managing director Mike Bennett says, 'We give people their own time and space to do with whatever they want but plan several team activities around them. For example, we try to make sure we all eat together of an evening, go on a tour together and, in the case of Dubai, go sea-fishing together.'

Joe Thorne was on E3's last event to Las Vegas. 'As a recent graduate I found the whole experience extremely beneficial,' he says. 'We all partied together and recovered with hangovers from hell around the pool. We bonded massively as a team. But this didn't stop after we touched down at Heathrow Airport. Far from it – the buzz, the memories and the experience lasted for months.'

LANGUAGE STUDY

Dependent prepositions

1 You need to use a particular preposition after many verbs, nouns and adjectives. Look at these extracts from the text on page 79 and identify which of the phrases in bold are:

1 verb + preposition 2 noun + preposition 3 adjective + preposition

a *Many employers see the annual team-building event as the (1)* ***makings of*** *a tight ship in their organisation.*

b *Normally (2)* ***aiming for*** *an eclectic (3)* ***mixture of*** *fun, focus and forward-vision, team awaydays are intended to be more than (4)* ***splattering*** *your colleagues* ***in*** *paint and listening to management-speak, which has little (5)* ***impact on*** *your role once back in the workplace.*

c *Well, yes, according to David Evans, chief executive of a company which (6)* ***specialises in*** *improving the performance of other organisations.*

d *Team bonding exercises are not just an (7)* ***excuse for*** *having a company knees-up.*

e *One of the many tasks Barber (8)* ***participated in*** *was a tandem biking exercise.*

f *It made us (9)* ***aware of*** *timing, control, and ultimately how to delegate, and say no!*

g *Team-building days are great for those (10)* ***interested in*** *trying something new.*

2 When a verb, noun or adjective + preposition is followed by a verb, what form does that verb usually take?

Grammar reference page 91

3 Complete these questions using the correct preposition from those given.

Example: *What are you responsible for at work?*

1 What are you responsible		at work?
2 Do you specialise	about	anything at work?
3 How much holiday are you entitled	for	each year?
4 Did you find it difficult to adapt	from	your job when you first started?
5 Is your job in any way different	in	how you imagined it would be?
6 Is your work compatible	into	studying?
7 Do you ever have to translate things	of	or from English at work?
8 Do you ever get fed up	to	your job?
9 What aspects	with	your job are the most difficult?
10 What are the best and worst things		your job?

4 Think about your job or a job you've had (this could be a part-time or weekend job). Work in groups and discuss some of the questions in Ex 3. If you have never had a job, find someone who has and ask them the questions.

5 Complete these newspaper headlines by adding the correct preposition.

1 New search engine to focus ______ teenage market

2 Eligibility ______ citizenship depends ______ wealth says report

3 FIFA suspicious ______ nil-nil draw

4 Area equivalent ______ that of UK destroyed every year

5 Moonbase agreement ______ US and Europe reached

6 Software giant split ______ two separate entities

7 Car manufacturers forced to comply ______ new emission rules

8 Lack ______ support blamed ______ club's bankruptcy

Are you a team player?

Listening

1 What happens if somebody has a problem at your place of work or study? What problems are common? How can they be tackled?

2 10 Listen to the radio programme. Where do Maria and Ethan work? What are their problems?

3 Listen again. How do Maria and Ethan introduce their problem? What phrases do they use to express dissatisfaction? Complete the extracts from the programme.

Maria:

1 ________________ I work with someone who is always really rude when I ask a question or make a suggestion.

2 Her whole attitude is one of non-cooperation and I've __________ of it.

3 I'm __________ all the friction. It's really __________.

Ethan:

1 I'd like ________________ with my new supervisor. She's determined to ________________.

2 She constantly has to know my whereabouts … I think she's __________.

3 It's put me ________________. I can't afford to leave … but I ________________.

4 Which of these things are advice to Maria and which to Ethan? Look at listening script 10 on page 95 and decide. Then underline the phrases Liz uses to give advice.

1 Have you tried approaching your colleague directly?

2 Then if nothing changes, you should think about going to the company's legal department.

3 And rather than making assumptions or placing blame, I recommend you begin the conversation by asking questions.

4 You don't have to meet with her alone; ask her manager or someone from the personnel department to be present.

5 If you're willing to talk with this person – and I think you should do so – then, it's a good idea to consider an approach that won't put your colleague on the defensive.

6 Talking over lunch, or away from your work environment might help.

7 My advice is, speak to her and ask her about the issues she has with you.

5 What do you think of Liz's advice? What would you have suggested? Tell the class.

Writing

1 Work in groups. Write your own 'Dear Liz' phone-in about difficult colleagues. Make up characters and problems. Use the language in Listening Ex 3 and 4.

2 Give your programme to another group to act out to the class. Which programme was most interesting / entertaining / useful / …?

Speaking

1 Are you a team player or a leader? Do the quiz on page 93. Then ask and answer the questions with a partner and note down your partner's answers.

2 Check your partner's score on page 96. Then discuss the results with your partner.

3 Look at the phrases in **bold** from the quiz analysis. Discuss their meaning with the class. Then work with a partner and answer the questions.

1 Do you like to **take the initiative** or prefer others to take it?

2 Is it important for you to **seek approval**?

3 Do you **confront conflict** or avoid it?

4 Do you **have high expectations** of yourself?

5 Do you think it's important that people **realise their potential**?

6 Do you prefer to **implement decisions** or make them?

CD-ROM For more activities go to **Groups Unit 4**

5 Review

Lead-in **1** Discuss these questions.

1 What type of music is coming into fashion and going out of fashion?

2 What are the most popular types of music among people of different ages, such as teenagers, 30-somethings, your parents' generation?

3 Who is your favourite music group or artist? Work in pairs and tell each other about the following:

- the kind of music they play
- the group's line-up
- when you first heard them
- why you like them
- if you have ever seen them or if you think you ever will
- how often and when you tend to listen to them
- your favourite song or album by them
- if they remind you of a particular person, place or time

Speaking

I'd say ...

What it boils down to ...

I suppose you can say ...

What I mean is ...

What do you mean by ...?

As far as I'm concerned ...

So what you're saying is ...

1 Look at the attributes of a music group in Box A. Match them with adjectives in Box B that can be used to describe them.

A	B
• appearance and image • lifestyle and attitude • live performance • lyrics • voice / singing • music • musicians and musicianship	captivating, charismatic, colourful, danceable, dynamic, emotive, extravagant, glamourous, inimitable, inspirational, irreplaceable, meaningful, mellow, memorable, noisy, obscure, original, outlandish, outrageous, relatable, reputable, skilful, soulful, talented, unpredictable, upbeat

2 Work in groups. Discuss what makes a good music group and rank the attributes in Ex 1 in order of importance. Add your own ideas if you wish.

- Use examples of groups you know and the adjectives above to illustrate your ideas.
- You can use the phrases in the speech bubbles in your discussion to explain your viewpoint and to clarify understanding of other people's ideas.

3 Present and explain the final ranking of your group to the class.

You are what you listen to

1 Work with a partner and discuss these questions.

1 What kinds of music do you think the people in the pictures listen to?
2 Does your appearance reflect the kind of music you listen to? Has it ever done so?
3 What do you think a person's taste in music says about them?

2 **11** Research has shown a connection between the music someone likes and their personality type. Listen to the first part of a radio programme and answer these questions.

1 Who was the research conducted by?
2 How many people participated in the survey?
3 What was the key element of the research?
4 What did the research reveal about people who listen to:
a classical music? **b** pop and chart music? **c** rap and hip-hop?
5 In what way is there more to listening to music than just enjoying it?
6 What can be central to many people's way of life?

3 **12** Listen to the second part of the radio programme. What does the interviewer say about:

a people who organise their CDs carefully?
b people who organise their CDs randomly?
c new couples?

4 Listen again and complete these extracts with the phrases in the box.

and so on   and that sort of thing   or thereabouts   or so   or whatever   sort of

1 Some are alphabeticised or divided into genre __________________, or, and this is more common we found, more randomly arranged.
2 They have a __________________ music room, which has two walls totally filled with shelves of CDs.
3 I think they must have about a thousand between them __________________.
4 Now, she is clearly an extremely organised and reliable person, the kind who doesn't get parking tickets __________________.
5 It would be interesting … to see where they and their CDs are in another two years __________________.
6 They used it to 'check each other out' nearly twice as much as books, television or sport __________________.

5 In each of these extracts from the radio programme identify examples of ellipsis and substitution and say what has been omitted or substituted.

1 If you want to assess a person's character, a quick look through their music collection is one of the most reliable ways of doing so.
2 With some young people, music …is why they dress, have their hair and generally look the way they do.
3 Presenter: But isn't that just a way of asserting your identity?
Researcher: Well, to a certain extent, yes, I think it is.
4 She and her boyfriend … have not yet combined their collections. Why they haven't done so, I don't know.

6 Work with a partner and discuss these questions.

1 How do you organise your music?
2 What does this say about you?
3 Do you agree with the research findings?

7 What would be on your ten-track CD of favourite songs? Compare your ideas with a partner and explain why you have chosen the tracks.

Song

1 Read the factfile about the *Dandy Warhols* and answer these questions.

1. What is the significance of the following dates?
   a 1995 **b** 1997 **c** 2000 **d** 2001
2. How has the band's line-up changed?
3. Where do the band throw their parties and how did they end up with this place?
4. How was their 2003 album different from their other albums?
5. How well-known are they?

factfile

Formed in Portland, Oregon in 1994 the *Dandy Warhols* consist of members Courtney Taylor-Taylor (vocals, guitar), Zia McCabe (keyboards), Peter Loew (guitar), and Brent DeBoer (drums). They released their debut album, *Dandy's rule OK?*, in 1995, but it wasn't until the release of their second album, *Dandy Warhols come down* in 1997, which included their first hit single, that the group attained more widespread success, especially in Europe. After DeBoer replaced the band's original drummer, who left to pursue a DJ-ing career, the group released their third album, *Thirteen tales from urban Bohemia* to much acclaim in 2000. The track *Bohemian like you* received massive radio play and became a hit in several countries. The song appeared on numerous film and television soundtracks and was used to great effect in television advertising campaigns for Chrysler and Vodafone in 2001. With the money earned from these adverts the band bought part of an apartment block in their hometown, which they converted for use as film and music studios, as well as being somewhere for the band to throw parties. 2003 saw the release of the group's synth-heavy, 80s-influenced fourth album, after which the group returned to more guitar-driven songs with subsequent releases. Though worldwide recognition and commercial success still eludes the band, they have garnered a large cult following in many countries.

2 13 Listen to the song and answer these questions.

1. Who do you think the singer is talking to?
2. What do we learn about this person's:
   a car **b** hair **c** job **d** interest in music **e** diet **f** living arrangements

3 What things do the singer and the person he's talking to have in common?

Bohemian* like you

You got a great car
Yeah what's wrong with it today?
I used to have one too
Maybe I'll come and have a look
I really love your hairdo yeah
I'm glad you like mine too
See we're looking pretty cool
Will get ya

So what do you do?
Oh yeah I wait tables too
No I haven't heard your band
'Cos you guys are pretty new
But if you dig on vegan food
Well, come over to my work
I'll have 'em cook you something
That you'll really love

'Cos I like you
Yeah I like you
And I'm feeling so bohemian like you
Yeah I like you
Yeah I like you
And I feel whoa ooo

Wait
Who's that guy just hangin' at your pad
He's lookin' kinda bummed
Yeah you broke up that's too bad
I guess it's fair if he always pays the rent
And he doesn't get bent about
Sleeping on the couch when I'm there

Chorus

I'm getting wise and I'm feeling so bohemian like you
It's you that I want so please
Just a casual, casual easy thing
Is it, it is for me
And I like you
Yeah I like you
I like you, I like you …
And I feel

* Bohemian = living or behaving in an informal way considered typical of artists and writers.

4 Would you describe any aspect of your lifestyle or behaviour as bohemian?

Vocabulary

1 Read How to play 'Question time' and play the game.

Question time

How to play

1. Play in two teams. You need a coin and each team needs a counter.
2. Each team puts its counter on the 'start' square. Team A tosses the coin and moves one square for heads and two squares for tails. Team B chooses one of the alternatives from the square and asks Team A the question for that colour category. Example for square 1: Name something you can shun.
3. Team A gives their answer. If Team B agrees the answer is correct, Team A can play next time. If the answer is incorrect, Team A misses a turn.
4. Team B now plays and so on.

Name something you can ...	What are you doing if you are ...	Give an adjective made from the word ...	Which preposition most commonly goes with ...

start

1 tackle / shun	2 bonding with someone / having a knees up	3 utilise / enhance	4 reputation / stop	5 focus / translate
6 adopt / implement	7 advantage / room	8 causing a scene / giving somebody a look	9 figure out / get across	10 specialise / participate
11 be hooked on / face up to	12 comply / benefit	13 enduring something / mucking in	14 explain / cure	15 be entitled / be aware
16 conduct / administer	17 delegating / confronting someone	18 value / size	19 being hands on / out of line	20 slug / number

finish

Extra practice

Unit 1

1 Complete the phrases in *italics*. The first letter of the missing word is given.

1 We all do our fair share of housework. Everyone has to *m* __________ *in*.

2 Mum does an awful lot and never complains. She really does *suffer in s* __________ some of the time.

3 Mum doesn't really *lose her t* __________, but you know when you're *out of l* __________ 'cos she'll *give you a l* __________.

4 Dad looked after us all loads when we were babies. He was very *h* __________ *on*.

2 Look at this data about the family in Europe. Examples of ellipsis are numbered 1–9. What information has been omitted in each case?

1	birth rate	6	__________
2	__________	7	__________
3	__________	8	__________
4	__________	9	__________
5	__________		

The European country with the highest birth rate is Ireland while Germany has the lowest (1).

There are about 5 million babies born in Europe each year, with around one third (2) born outside marriage. The largest proportions of births outside marriage (over 50%) are found in Estonia and Sweden, and the lowest (3) in Cyprus and Greece.

Two thirds of European households are without children. The proportion of households with one child is 16%, 13% (4) have two children and 4% (5) 3 or more (6).

Single-parent households represent 13% of all households in Europe. At 24%, the United Kingdom has the highest rate (7) in Europe.

Cyprus and Denmark have the highest marriage rates in Europe while Slovenia has the lowest (8). The European countries with the highest divorce rates are the Czech Republic and Lithuania, while the lowest (9) are found in Ireland, Italy and Greece.

3 The following sentences contain examples of ellipsis and substitution. Complete them so they are true for you.

Example: I'd love to *be able to take a few days off*, but I just can't at the moment.

1 I'd love to __________, but I just can't at the moment.

2 I've never __________, but I'd like to one day.

3 Most of my friends __________, but I don't.

4 I __________, but I wish I hadn't.

5 I once __________, but I'll never do so again.

6 I didn't __________, but I should have.

4 What has been substituted in each quote? Which quote do you like the best? ☐

Example:

Any American who is prepared to run for president should automatically, by definition, be disqualified from ever *doing so*. (Gore Vidal, US author & dramatist, 1925–) *running for president*

1 Human beings, who are almost unique in having the ability to learn from the experience of others, are also remarkable for their apparent disinclination to *do so*. (Douglas Adams British science fiction novelist, 1952–2001) __________

2 The definition of genius is that it acts unconsciously; and those who have produced immortal works, have *done so* without knowing how or why. (William Hazlitt, English essayist, 1778–1830) __________

3 The wise man thinks about his troubles only when there is some purpose in *doing so*; at other times he thinks about other things. (Bertrand Russell, British author and philosopher, 1872–1970) __________

5 Complete these headlines with the verbs in the box.

adopt	conduct	establish
preserve	prohibit	register

1 **All countries to __________ single currency**

2 **US military to __________ human cloning tests**

3 **Scientists __________ direct link between diet and longevity**

4 **EU to __________ all cigarette advertising**

5 **All nations agree to __________ existing rainforest**

6 **All adults to __________ their religion according to new law**

Unit 2

1 Replace the underlined words by completing the euphemisms.

1 He's really mean.
c________ w________ m________

2 My parents are really old.
g________ o________ a b________

3 She's poor. She struggles to pay the bills.
o________ a l________ i________

4 He's really fat.
o________ t________ l________ s________

5 My friend's car is falling to bits.
h________ s________ b________ d________

6 He drinks a lot when he goes out.
l________ a t________

2 Look at these definitions of adjectives ending in *-able* that are made from the words in the box. Write each adjective in the appropriate space. You will need to add a negative prefix in some cases.

admire	change	~~imagine~~	knowledge
laugh	question	replace	understand

1 Very difficult to imagine: *an agreement between the two countries is unimaginable*
2 Possibly not true, accurate or complete: *the results of the test seem highly* ________
3 Normal and reasonable in a particular situation: *their reaction is perfectly* ________ *in the circumstances*
4 Valuable or rare and impossible to replace if used, lost or destroyed: *an* ________ *collection of jewellery*
5 Very silly or unreasonable: *his claims are* ________
6 Knowing a lot about many different subjects or about one particular subject: *he's extremely* ________ *about business and finance*
7 Tending to change suddenly and often: *a period of rather* ________ *weather*
8 Deserving to be admired or respected: *an* ________ *objective*

3 Complete these news report extracts with an adjective ending in *-able* formed from the words in *italics*. You will need to use a negative prefix in some cases.

1 The law now demands a total ban in all public places, something which was ________ only a few years ago. *think*
2 The contribution made by every member is ________ and this is the key to their phenomenal chart success. *value*
3 It does not live up to the hype by any means, but is pleasantly ________ nevertheless. *watch*
4 His is one of the most ________ faces on the planet. *recognise*
5 An ________ return of service clinched the game and the second set. *stop*
6 You are angry that you have lost your money and two hours out of your life watching this ________ horror. *speak*
7 The assertion that the attacks were not ________ remains ________. *prevent question*
8 There is no doubt that ________ sums of undeclared money are regularly changing hands between clubs and agents, a situation that FIFA has condemned as '________ and ________'. The governing body has also made it clear that such illegal dealings are not by any means confined to the less ________ agents. *size accept excuse reputation*

4 What or who do you think each of the news extracts in Ex 3 is about?

1 Example: smoking
2 ________
3 ________
4 ________
5 ________
6 ________
7 ________
8 ________

5 Put an appropriate ending on these words to make them into adjectives.

1 colour*ful*
2 child____
3 harm____
4 care____
5 advantage____
6 harm____
7 dust____
8 mist____
9 meaning____
10 fool____
11 hair____
12 snob____
13 mood____
14 rock____

6 Complete these sentences with an adjective formed from the words in the box.

danger	room	slug	thought

1 Don't worry, he isn't ________.

2 My computer is a bit ________ today.

3 Thank you. That's very ________ of you.

4 It's very ________ in the back.

Unit 3

1 Complete these email extracts with an appropriate form of the phrasal verbs in the box.

be on about boil down to figure out get across point out

1 As well as the problems with the computer already mentioned, I would also like to ________________ the extremely poor customer service on your help-line.

2 Most of the time, I couldn't ________________ what your 'agents' were saying. To be honest, most of the time I just didn't have a clue what they ________________.

3 I just didn't seem to be able to ______________ to them that I'd already tried the things they were suggesting and that they didn't seem to understand my problem. I guess it just ________ __________ the fact that they're not actually that knowledgeable or well-trained.

2 Match the phrases to the correct endings in both groups.

1 What I'm	a mean by …?
2 What do you	b saying is …
3 If I've understood you	c getting at is …
4 What I'm trying to	d say is …
5 So, what you're	e correctly, …
6 To put it	f me?
7 Are you with	g follow?
8 Do you	h a different way
9 Do you see what I	i saying?
10 What are you	j mean?

3 Which of the phrases in Ex 2 would be used by

1 the speaker [1] [ ] [ ] [ ] [ ] [ ]

2 the listener [ ] [ ] [ ] [ ]

4 Complete the sentences using an appropriate question word combined with the suffix *-ever*, for example *whatever*.

1 I like all computer games – races, shoot 'em ups, role-play, ____________.

2 We can go anywhere you like – Fifth Avenue, Central Park, the Statue of Liberty, ____________.

3 I don't mind how we get there – taxi, car, walk, ____________.

4 Invite who you like – friends, colleagues, classmates, ____________.

5 Call round anytime – seven, eight, ____________.

6 Stay as long as you like – a couple of days, a week, ____________.

5 Rewrite these email extracts by putting the words and phrases in *italics* in an appropriate position.

Example:

So, how's it going now you've moved in together, settling down? We really must meet up and have a good catch up. *and all that* *sometime*

So, how's it going now you've moved in together, settling down <u>and all that</u>? We really must meet up <u>sometime</u> and have a good catch up.

1 Mel from the London office has sent me an attachment in a compressed format. She said I needed some 'unzipper' program and emailed it to me, but I just don't know what I'm doing with this. Can you have a look at it for me? *sort of* *kind of thing*

2 I really like the new job. Most of the time it's sorting out error messages. It's just the challenge I really enjoy. *and the like* *kind of*

3 You're welcome to come and stay one or two nights anytime you like. We've got a spare room-cum-study you can stay in. *or whatever* *sort of*

4 Maria's away at the moment, so I'm spending my time eating take-away pizza and watching all my old favourite DVDs, you know, 101 Best World Cup goals, 101 Funniest TV moments. You should come round before she's back. *and that sort of thing* *sometime*

6 Answer these questions about yourself with the phrases in the box.

Example: *three years more or less* *1 metre 70-ish*

getting on for give or take -ish more or less or so or thereabouts

1 How long have you been learning English?

____

2 How long have you lived in your house?

____

3 How long have you had a computer?

____

4 What time do you generally go to bed?

____

5 How tall are you?

____

6 How much money have you got on you?

____

Unit 4

1 Complete the following article about leadership with an appropriate form of the verbs in the boxes.

I'm in charge

implement run

At it's most basic level leadership involves (1) ___________ meetings effectively, keeping the team informed and (2) ___________ and explaining decisions.

bond enhance realise utilise

At mid-level, it includes ensuring that a team (3) ___________ and (4) ___________ team performance. This is done by creating the right conditions to (5) ___________ team members' individual skills and to enable the team to (6) ___________ its potential fully.

face up to perform set tackle take

Top-level leaders (7) ___________ challenges, (8) ___________ problems head on and (9) ___________ initiative. In doing so they act as role models and inspire confidence in the team. At the top level, leadership is about (10) ___________ standards and making sure that people (11) ___________ to that level.

2 Which preposition goes with each set of words and phrases? Use a different preposition for each set.

specialise participate believe be lacking be fluent	*in*
worry reminisce have doubts be nervous	
comply be fed up be compatible be popular	

adapt be equivalent be entitled be related be similar	
have impact depend concentrate put the blame	
benefit suffer deviate be different	

be aware be typical be envious a mixture a lack	
translate split divide change	
apologise be eligible be famous be responsible	

3 Complete these sentence beginnings with your own ideas.

Example: I'm envious *of people who can play the piano.*

1 I'm envious ___________
2 I'm (not) fluent ___________
3 I'm similar ___________
4 I'm different ___________
5 I often reminisce ___________
6 I (don't) have (any) doubts ___________
7 I'm (not) eligible ___________
8 I (don't) think I have the makings ___________

4 Match the halves of these work-related quotes.

1 ___ 2 ___ 3 ___ 4 ___ 5 ___ 6 ___ 7 ___

1 The world is divided
2 To manage a system effectively, you might focus
3 Any corporate policy and plan which is typical
4 Don't worry
5 Everyone is entitled
6 One of the penalties for refusing to participate
7 A young man … should look for the single spark of individuality that makes him different

a in politics is that you end up being governed by your inferiors. (Plato, Greek philosopher, 427–347 BC)
b to be stupid, but some abuse the privilege. (Anonymous)
c of the industry is doomed to mediocrity. (Bruce Henderson, management consultant, 1915–1992)
d on the interactions of the parts rather than their behaviour taken separately. (Russell L. Ackoff, academic and author, 1919–)
e from other folks, and develop that for all he is worth. (Henry Ford, automobile industrialist, 1863–1947)
f into people who do things and people who get the credit. (Dwight Morrow, businessman, politician, and diplomat, 1873–1931)
g about people stealing an idea. If it's original, you will have to ram it down their throats. (Howard Aiken, computer scientist, 1900–1973)

Grammar reference

Unit 1

Ellipsis and substitution

In speaking and writing we generally provide only as much information as is necessary to convey what we want to express. This involves leaving out or replacing words and phrases to avoid repetition.

Ellipsis

Textual ellipsis occurs in both speaking and writing. Words are missed out in grammatically predictable sentence positions. It often occurs after *and*, *but* and *because* etc.

Most of my friends love going clubbing, but I don't (love going clubbing).
I didn't go out last night because I didn't want to (go out last night).
We'd love to get away for a few days, but we just can't (get away for a few days) *at the moment.*
Pete's got ten pounds and I've got twenty (pounds).

Situational ellipsis occurs mainly in speaking. The context makes it clear what is missing.
Feeling better? (~~Are you~~ feeling better?)
A: *Going to the party?* (~~Are you~~ going to the party?)
B: *Possibly.* (~~I am~~ possibly ~~going to the party~~)
A: *When you back?* (When ~~are~~ you ~~coming~~ back?)
B: *Friday.* (~~We are coming back on~~ Friday)

Substitution

Substitution refers to the words we use (*so, do, did*, etc) that replace words we have omitted.
Do, does, did etc replaces a verb clause.

It is usually used in conjunction with *so* when referring to voluntary or deliberate actions and when referring to the same subject as previously mentioned.

We'll get married one day, but we're not planning on ***doing so*** *just yet.* (getting married)

I once did a bungee jump, but I'll never ***do so*** *again.* (do a bungee jump)

I didn't see the incident, but it seems that everyone else ***did***. (saw the incident)
I thought it would rain, and ***so*** *it has* (... and it has rained)
A: *Is Dave coming with us?*
B: *I think* ***so***. (I think that Dave is coming with us)
A: *It wasn't Carlos who called.*
B: *I thought* ***not***. (I thought it wasn't Carlos who called)

Unit 2

Forming adjectives from verbs and nouns (adjective suffixes)

-able

The suffix *-able* can be added to:

- certain verbs to make adjectives describing something that can or can't be done.
  His reaction was totally predictable.
  Lampard's penalty kick was unstoppable.
- certain nouns to make adjectives describing a quality that something has.
  She's very knowledgeable about art.
  Thanks for your invaluable help.

-ible

-ible is a less common alternative to *-able*. There is no simple rule to tell you which words take *-ible* and you need to learn them individually.
They said that it was indestructible.
His behaviour is indefensible.

There are a few common 'irregular' adjectives that end in *-able* or *-ible*.

inexplicable	(you can't explain it)
appreciable	(enough to be noticed/appreciated)
reputable	(has a good reputation)
(il)legible	(you can('t) read it)
(in)edible	(you can('t) eat it)
(in)visible	(you can('t) see it)
(in)audible	(you can('t) hear it)
(in)credible	(you can('t) believe it)
(im)plausible	(difficult to accept as true)

Negative prefixes

Many adjectives ending in *-able* or *-ible* take negative prefixes. The most common negative prefixes used in this way are *un-*, *in-* and *non-*. You need to learn how to form the negative of words as you come across them.

You generally use *il-* for words beginning with *l*, *im-* for words beginning with *m* and *p*, and *ir-* for those beginning with *r*.
illegible illegal immovable immature impenetrable irreplaceable irregular

-y / -ful / -ish / -ous

You can form adjectives from nouns using the suffixes *-y*, *-ful*, *-ish*, and *-ous*.
The meaning is 'having the quality of'

It's been a bit cloudy over the last few days.
India is such a colourful country.
He's very childish.
Speaking a foreign language can be very advantageous for work.

Unit 3

Using vague language

You can use the following phrases to express the idea of 'similarity' to what you have previously mentioned.

and stuff   and / or whatever   and all that   and the like   and that kind / sort of thing / stuff   and so on

I don't really like rap and hip-hop and that kind of stuff.
I love going out clubbing and all that.
We've got all we need here – shops, bars, convenient public transport and so on.

a / some kind of and *a / some sort of* express 'something similar to'
I've got some kind of virus on my computer.
I've got a sort of office at home where I work.

-ever

The suffix *-ever* can be combined with question words to give the meaning 'It doesn't matter which / who / when' etc.

We can leave whenever you like.
I don't mind what we eat – Indian, Chinese, whatever.
Help yourself to anything – food, there's beer in the fridge, DVDs, whatever you want.

Approximating

You can use the following phrases to give approximations.

about   around   getting on for   give or take   -ish   in the region of   more or less   or so   or thereabouts

It's worth in the region of £250,000.
He must be getting on for 40 I'd say.
I'll be there around six-ish.
I've got about 100 CDs or thereabouts.
I'd say he's about 1 metre 80 or so.

Unit 4

Dependent prepositions with verbs, nouns and adjectives

You need to use a particular preposition after certain verbs, nouns and adjectives. Often this preposition is just a linking word, which contributes no meaning.

There are no rules about which prepositions to use with which words and you need to learn which preposition to use as you come across new words. Try to remember the word and the preposition as one item of language, for example '*aim for*', '*specialise in*' etc.

Here are some of the more common verb, noun or adjective + preposition structures.

verb + preposition

aim for   accuse of   adapt to   apologise for   approve of   believe in   benefit from   blame for   complain to / about   comply with   concentrate on   congratulate on   connect to   consist of   cover in   depend on   divide into   dream about / of   embark on / upon   be entitled to   excuse for   expose to   focus on   forgive for   insist on   look forward to   object to   participate in   prevent from   react to   rely on   specialise in   split into   succeed in   think about / of   translate into   worry about

The document needs ***translating into*** *English.*
Don't ***worry about*** *me.*
Can we ***focus on*** *the facts?*
He's someone you can always ***rely on****.*

noun + preposition

advantage of   agreement between   alternative to   aspect of   attitude towards   cause of   contact with   cost of   damage to   decrease / increase in   demand for   difference between   eligibility for   the equivalent of   example of   excuse for   experience of   exposure to   demand for   impact on   lack of   mixture of   need for   participation in   photograph of   reaction to   reason for   relationship with   rise / fall in   rule about   solution to   trouble with

Was there much ***damage to*** *the car?*
Have you made ***contact with*** *anyone yet?*
The ***demand for*** *CD players is decreasing all the time.*
Is there any ***advantage of*** *going first.*
I'm having some ***trouble with*** *my computer.*

adjective + preposition

accustomed to   afraid of   allergic to   angry with   aware of   certain about   compatible with   covered in   dependent on   different from   equivalent to   famous / well-known for   interested in   fed up with   fond of   good / bad / useless / terrible at   keen on   lacking in   late for   optimistic about   proud of   ready for   reliant on   responsible for   serious about   sorry for   superstitious about   suspicious of   used to

I'm ***allergic to*** *dairy products.*
One Euro is ***equivalent to*** *about 70 pence.*
Is it ***compatible with*** *Windows Vista?*
There have been no problems that I'm ***aware of****.*

When a verb directly follows a verb, noun or adjective + preposition, you use the *-ing* form of this verb.

I'm ***thinking of*** *joining a gym.*
Are you ***serious about*** *joining the police?*
What's his ***excuse for*** *being late?*
I'm not really ***used to*** *driving on the left yet.*

GROUPS

Wordlist

*** the 2,500 most common English words, ** very common words, * fairly common words

Unit 1

administer *v* /ədˈmɪnɪstə/
adopt *v* /əˈdɒpt/ ***
bereavement *n* /bɪˈri:vmənt/
broody *adj* /ˈbru:di/
close *adj* /kləʊs/ ***
conduct *v* /kənˈdʌkt/ ***
devote (your) life to *phr* /dɪˌvəʊt (jɔ:) ˈlaɪf tə/
elated *adj* /ɪˈleɪtɪd/
elitist *adj* /ɪˈli:tɪst/
establish *v* /ɪˈstæblɪʃ/ ***
get on like a house on fire *expr* /get ˌɒn laɪk ə ˈhaʊs ɒn ˌfaɪə/
get on the property ladder *expr* /ˌget ɒn ðə ˈprɒpəti ˌlædə/
give and take *phr* /ˌgɪv ən ˈteɪk/
give sb a look *phr* /ˌgɪv … ə ˈlʊk/
give up hope *phr* /ˌgɪv ʌp ˈhəʊp/
hands on *adj* /ˌhændz ˈɒn/
hands off *adj* /ˌhændz ˈɒf/
If nature has its way *expr* /ɪf ˌneɪtʃə ˌhæz ɪts ˈweɪ/
ignore *v* /ɪgˈnɔ:/ **
lawless *adj* /ˈlɔ:ləs/
lose (your) temper *expr* /ˌlu:z (jɔ:) ˈtempə/
motley group *n* /ˈmɒtli ˌgru:p/
muck in *v* /ˌmʌk ˈɪn/
nag *v* /næg/
neglect *v* /nɪˈglekt/ **
nowhere near as … as *expr* /ˌnəʊweə ˈnɪər əz … əz/
order *n* /ˈɔ:də/ ***
out of line *adj* /ˌaʊt əv ˈlaɪn/
preserve *v* /prɪˈzɜ:v/ ***
progressive *adj* /prəʊˈgresɪv/ **
prohibit *v* /prəʊˈhɪbɪt/ *
register *v* /ˈredʒɪstə/ ***
resent *v* /rɪˈzent/
scourge *n* /skɜ:dʒ/ *
shun *v* /ʃʌn/
squabble *v* /ˈskwɒbl/
stick up for sb *expr* /ˌstɪk ˈʌp fə/
suffer in silence *phr* /ˌsʌfər ɪn ˈsaɪləns/
the icing on the cake *expr* /ði ˌaɪsɪŋ ɒn ðə ˈkeɪk/
the patience of a saint *phr* /ðə ˌpeɪʃəns əv ə ˈseɪnt/
tied down *adj* /ˌtaɪd ˈdaʊn/
trespass *v* /ˈtrespəs/
uniqueness *n* /ju:ˈni:knəs/
wishful thinking *phr* /ˌwɪʃfl ˈθɪŋkɪŋ/

Unit 2

advantageous *adj* /ˌædvənˈteɪdʒəs/
adventurous *adj* /ədˈventʃərəs/
advisable *adj* /ədˈvaɪzəbl/
appreciable *adj* /əˈpri:ʃəbl/
at any rate *phr* /ət ˈeni ˌreɪt/
be between jobs (right now) *phr* /bɪ bɪˌtwi:n ˈdʒɒbz (raɪt ˌnaʊ)/
be getting on a bit *expr* /bɪ ˌgetɪŋ ˈɒn ə ˌbɪt/
be on a low income *phr* /bi ˌɒn ə ˌləʊ ˈɪŋkʌm/
be very careful with money *phr* /bɪ ˌveri ˌkeəfl wɪð ˈmʌni/
But on the other hand, *expr* /bət ˌɒn ði ˈʌðə ˌhænd/
childish *adj* /ˈtʃaɪldɪʃ/ *
doable *adj* /ˈdu:əbl/
downloadable *adj* /ˌdaʊnˈləʊdəbl/
dusty *adj* /ˈdʌsti/ *
foolish *adj* /ˈfu:lɪʃ/ *
hairy *adj* /ˈheəri/ *
harmful *adj* /ˈhɑ:mfl/ *
I suppose you can say (that) … *phr* /aɪ səˈpəʊz jə kən ˌseɪ (ðət)/
in a way *phr* /ˌɪn ə ˈweɪ/
incurable *adj* /ɪnˈkjʊərəbl/
indescribable *adj* /ˌɪndɪˈskraɪbəbl/
inescapable *adj* /ɪnɪˈskeɪpəbl/
inexplicable *adj* /ɪnɪksˈplɪkəbl/
irretrievable *adj* /ˌɪrəˈtri:vəbl/
justifiable *adj* /ˈdʒʌstɪˌfaɪəbl/
kind of *phr* /ˈkaɪnd əv/
knowledgeable *adj* /ˈnɒlɪdʒəbl/
like a tipple *phr* /ˌlaɪk ə ˈtɪpl/
mentally challenged *adj* /ˌmentəli ˈtʃælɪndʒd/
misty *adj* /ˈmɪsti/
moody *adj* /ˈmu:di/
morally different *adj* /ˌmɒrəli ˈdɪfrənt/
motivationally deficient *adj* /məʊtɪˌveɪʃnəli dɪˈfɪʃnt/
need to go to the bathroom *phr* /ˌni:d tə ˌgəʊ tə ðə ˈbɑ:θru:m/
numerous *adj* /ˈnju:mərəs/ **
on the large side /ɒn ðə ˈlɑ:dʒ saɪd/
reputable *adj* /ˈrepjʊtəbl/
rocky *adj* /ˈrɒki/ *
roomy *adj* /ˈru:mi/
salty *adj* /ˈsɔ:lti/
sheepish *adj* /ˈʃi:pɪʃ/
sizeable *adj* /ˈsaɪzəbl/
sluggish *adj* /ˈslʌgɪʃ/
snobbish *adj* /ˈsnɒbɪʃ/
sort of *phr* /ˈsɔ:t əv/
sth has seen better days *expr* /… həz ˌsi:n ˌbetə ˈdeɪz/
unavoidable *adj* /ˌʌnəˈvɔɪdəbl/
under the circumstances *phr* /ˌʌndə ðə ˈsɜ:kəmstɑ:nsɪz/
unspeakable *adj* /ʌnˈspi:kəbl/
unstoppable *adj* /ʌnˈstɒpəbl/
vertically challenged *adj* /ˌvɜ:tɪkli ˈtʃælɪndʒd/

Unit 3

amount to *v* /əˈmaʊnt tə/ **
and all that *phr* /ənd ˌɔ:l ˈðæt/
and stuff *phr* /ən ˈstʌf/
and that sort of thing *phr* /ən ˈðæt ˌsɔ:t əv ˌθɪŋ/
and the like *phr* /ən ðə ˈlaɪk/
Are you with me? *expr* /ə jə ˈwɪð ˌmi:/
average *adj* /ˈævərɪdʒ/ ***
be getting at *v* /bɪ ˈgetɪŋ ˌæt/
be on about *v* /bi ˈɒn əˌbaʊt/
boil down to *v* /ˌbɔɪl ˈdaʊn tu:/
convey *v* /kənˈveɪ/ **
Do you follow? *phr* /də jə ˈfɒləʊ/
Do you get me? *expr* /də jə ˈget ˌmi:/
figure out *v* /ˌfɪgər ˈaʊt/
focus on *v* /ˈfəʊkəs ˌɒn/ ***
get sth across *v* /ˌget … əˈkrɒs/
getting on for … *expr* /ˌgetɪŋ ɒn fə (fɔ)/
give or take *expr* /ˈgɪv ɔ: ˌteɪk/
hooked on *adj* /ˈhʊkt ɒn/
however (long) *phr* /haʊˈevə (ˌlɒŋ)/
I suppose I'm really saying … *phr* /aɪ səˌpəʊz aɪm ˈrɪəli ˌseɪɪŋ/
In other words, you … *phr* /ɪn ˈʌðə ˌwɜ:dz ju:/
in the region of *phr* /ˈɪn ðə ˌri:dʒn əv/
(50)ish *adj* /(ˈfɪfti)ˌɪʃ/
more or less *phr* /ˌmɔ:r ɔ: ˈles/
or so *phr* /ˌɔ: ˈsəʊ/
or thereabouts *phr* /ɔ: ˌðeərəˈbaʊts/
point out *v* /ˌpɔɪnt ˈaʊt/
respondent *n* /rɪˈspɒndənt/
retrieve *v* /rɪˈtri:v/ *
So what you're trying to say is … *phr* /ˌsəʊ ˈwɒt jɔ: ˌtraɪɪŋ tə ˌseɪ ɪz/
To put it a different way *phr* /tə ˌpʊt ɪt ə ˈdɪfrənt ˌweɪ/
track *v* /træk/ *
What do you mean by …? *phr* /ˈwɒt də jə ˌmi:n baɪ/
What I'm getting at is … *expr* /ˌwɒt aɪm ˈgetɪŋ æt ɪz/
whatever *pron* /wɒtˈevə/ ***
whenever *pron* /wenˈevə/ **
wherever *pron* /weərˈevə/ **
whoever *pron* /hu:ˈevə/ **

Unit 4

a return on the investment *phr* /ə rɪˌtɜ:n ɒn ði ɪnˈvestmənt/
a tight ship *expr* /ə ˌtaɪt ˈʃɪp/
adapt to *v* /əˈdæpt tə/ **
aspect of sth *n* /ˈæspekt əv/ ***
awayday *n* /əˈweɪdeɪ/
not be seen dead *expr* /ˌnɒt bɪ ˌsi:n ˈded/
be tired of *expr* /bɪ ˈtaɪəd əv/
best / worst thing (about sth) *n* /ˈbest, ˈwɜ:st θɪŋ (əˌbaʊt)/
bond *v* /bɒnd/
chief executive *n* /tʃi:f ɪgˈzekjʊtɪv/ *
compatible with *adj* /kəmˈpætəbl wɪð/ *
comply *v* /kəmˈplaɪ/ **
confront conflict *phr* /kənˌfrʌnt ˈkɒnflɪkt/
delegate *v* /ˈdeləgeɪt/ *
eclectic *adj* /ɪˈklektɪk/
enhance *v* /ɪnˈhɑ:ns/ **
entitled to *adj* /ɪnˈtaɪtld tu:/ ***
entity *n* /ˈentəti/ **
face up to *v* /ˈfeɪs ˌʌp tə/
fed up with *adj* /ˌfed ˈʌp wɪð/
get sb down *expr* /ˌget … ˈdaʊn/
get up close and personal *phr* /ˌget ʌp ˌkləʊs ən ˈpɜ:snəl/
hangover *n* /ˈhæŋəʊvə/
have enough of sth / it *expr* /hæv ɪˈnʌf əv/
have high expectations *phr* /hæv ˌhaɪ ekspekˈteɪʃnz/
Have you tried (+ -ing)? *phr* /həv jə ˌtraɪd/
I can't stand (+ -ing) *expr* /aɪ ˌkɑ:nt ˌstænd/
I recommend you (+ inf) *phr* /aɪ ˌrekəmend ju:/
I'd like your advice on *phr* /aɪd ˌlaɪk jɔ:r ədˌvaɪs ɒn/
impact *n* /ˈɪmpækt/ ***
implement decisions *phr* /ˌɪmplɪˌment dɪˈsɪʒnz/
leave sth at the door *expr* /ˌli:v … ət ðə dɔ:/
literally *adv* /ˈlɪtərəli/ **
make sb's life a misery *phr* /ˌmeɪk … ˌlaɪf ə ˈmɪzəri/
menial *adj* /ˈmi:niəl/
(-ing) might help *phr* /… maɪt ˌhelp/
My advice is *phr* /ˈmaɪ ədˌvaɪs ɪs/
out of order *expr* /ˌaʊt əv ˈɔ:də/
participate *v* /pɑ:ˈtɪsɪˌpeɪt/ **
preconceived notion *n* /ˌpri:kənˌsi:vd ˈnəʊʃn/
proactively *adv* /prəʊˈæktɪvli/
put sb in a (real) dilemma *phr* /ˌpʊt … ɪn ə (ˌrɪəl) dɪˈlemə/
realise (your) potential *phr* /ˌrɪəˌlaɪz (jɔ:) pəˈtenʃl/
seek approval *phr* /ˌsi:k əˈpru:vl/
socialise with *v* /ˈsəʊʃəˌlaɪz wɪð/
specialise in *v* /ˈspeʃəˌlaɪz ɪn/ *
split *v* /splɪt/ **
tackle *v* /ˈtækl/ **
take the initiative *phr* /ˌteɪk ði ɪˈnɪʃətɪv/
the makings of *expr* /ðə ˈmeɪkɪŋz əv/
utilise *v* /ˈju:tɪlaɪz/
not what (you) bargain for *expr* /ˌnɒt ˌwɒt (ju:) ˈbɑ:gɪn fɔ:/
with an open mind *phr* /wɪð ən ˌəʊpən ˈmaɪnd/
You should think about (+ -ing) *phr* /jə ʃʊd ˌθɪŋk əbaʊt ˈ…/

Communication activities

Unit 1, Reading and vocabulary Ex 1 page 66

In 2004 the fertility rate in the UK was 1.77 children per woman. This was an increase from 1.71 in 2003 and a further increase from the record low of 1.63 in 2001. During the 1960s 'baby boom' the fertility rate peaked in 1964 at 2.95 children per woman. In 2004, the average age of women having their first birth was 27.1 years. Around one in five women currently reaching the end of their fertile life is childless.

(Source: National Statistics, www.statistics.gov.uk)

Unit 2, Speaking and pronunciation Ex 3 page 73

1 Read your rolecard for both situations.

2 Prepare notes to help you with your roles.

3 Do the role-plays with Student B. Include the phrases in Speaking and pronunciation Ex 1 and some of the euphemisms from page 70.

Rolecard 1

You lost your job a couple of months ago and have been holed up in your flat, eating fast food and watching TV. You feel very depressed and see no future for yourself. You have really let yourself go but you don't care. Student B is your friend and has come to visit you but you don't really want to see anybody.

Rolecard 2

Student B is your flatmate. A close friend has recently died and he / she is very upset. You sympathise but you need some money to pay the rent and the telephone bill. It is always a bit difficult getting money from your flatmate and the landlord has threatened to evict you over late payments. You suspect your flatmate is milking the situation to avoid paying but you don't want to lose him / her as a flatmate as you have a good relationship otherwise. Talk about the situation with him / her. Start like this: *Listen, I realise …*

Unit 4, Speaking Ex 1 page 81

Leadership quiz

1 How important is status to you?
- a Very important. I like to feel like I'm part of the elite.
- b Quite important. It's good to be in with the in-crowd.
- c It's more about the quality of relationships than where you fall within those relationships.
- d Not very important. I just want to get on.

2 In your childhood what was your 'gang rank'?
- a The leader; feared by all.
- b The funny one; adored by all.
- c The thinking one; listened to by all.
- d The geeky one; noticed by none.

3 At college or work do you come up with new ideas?
- a All the time. I let everyone know what I think.
- b Quite often, but not at all if it would mean upsetting someone.
- c Often: being careful of any personal and political issues.
- d Rarely: what if it was the wrong thing?

4 You have just faced some negative feedback. How do you respond?
- a Get angry and defensive.
- b Listen carefully but come away feeling disappointed.
- c Consider what you could change or improve.
- d Sigh and think, 'yeah that's me'.

5 Faced with a problem to solve, what do you do?
- a Come up with one solution and pronounce it correct.
- b Generate a few possible solutions and ask others what they think.
- c Brainstorm with a group of people.
- d Seek your tutor's or your manager's advice.

6 You have been asked to do something that is beyond your abilities. Do you …?
- a take it on energetically: you're up for anything.
- b give it your best shot, making a passing joke about not blaming you if it all goes wrong.
- c agree to do the task, but ask for further direction.
- d stress out and finally confess that you just don't think you could manage it.

7 Is delegation …
- a a waste of time: no one else will be able to do it as well as you so you might as well do it yourself.
- b an easy way to share the workload.
- c an effective way of creating new learning opportunities for others.
- d something you're always on the receiving end of.

8 Change to you means …
- a something to be controlled.
- b an opportunity where anything could happen.
- c a chance to make progress.
- d something to just go along with.

Listening scripts

Unit 1 Living together

Listening script 01

Reading text from page 67

Listening script 02

(P = presenter, R = Reporter)

P: Today on *Your Travel* Lisa Alexander reports on the colourful and controversial living community of Christiania in Copenhagen.

R: Copenhagen seems to epitomise the modern European capital and in many ways it does so.

But in the Christianshavn district lies a different kind of place – a motley group of hippies, artists and misfits have founded a home that shuns order, rules and conformity. The "freetown" of Christiania has been conducting a social experiment for more than 30 years. Fiercely independent-minded, the Christianite squatters have established their own holidays, government and rules.

The Christianites were determined to create a place where they could create art, let their children play in overgrown nature and live out untraditional lifestyles – and they did. Strange houses were erected. Cars were banned, and ecological experiments with wind and solar power, garbage recycling and water treatment took place before the rest of the country had even heard of the green movement.

A consensus democracy was formed, wherein no decision could be made without the agreement of all participants. There were no laws, only a few rules – paramount amongst them the prohibition on buying and selling property. Even now, Christianites do not own their homes. They have a close community and place a heavy value on community programs – feeding the homeless, creating their own kindergartens, playgrounds and clinics.

But many outside Christiania see the community as a scourge on the city, a group of drug-smoking criminals trespassing on public land and ignoring the laws the rest of Denmark have to obey. Liberal governments in the past adopted a hands-off policy but now the government is demanding changes. The dirt streets are to receive official names; buildings are to receive house numbers; and, residents will have to register where they live. In their words, the government wants to "normalise" the area.

Government officials claim the plan seeks to preserve the cultural uniqueness of the area, which attracts close to a million tourists a year, but private ownership of the land will need to be arranged. Christianites are demanding that a system of common ownership remains. In their eyes, all the things that have made the area so special are rooted in the unique way they administer the area and prohibit the buying and selling of homes.

No matter what the outcome of the negotiations, no amount of normalisation could ever make Christiania normal. Lawless, elitist and dirty? Or progressive, inventive and free? Whatever your opinion is of Copenhagen's most unique neighbourhood, it always leaves a lasting impression on visitors.

Unit 2 Talk talk

Listening script 03

Reading text from page 71

Listening script 04

(T = Tatyana, L = Lars, P = Paolo)

T: My name's Tatyana, I'm from Russia and I've been learning English in Oxford for about a year now. I'm planning to study international business and administration at an English university. I think it's difficult to get a good job without English – English is the world's *lingua franca*. I realise that some people don't like that, but under the circumstances, I tend to think it's unavoidable. I can't get a good job in my country if I don't learn English. Perhaps all countries should teach children English when they are small, so they find it easy to learn. I found English easy to learn at first, but then it got harder because the tenses are so difficult.

L: My name's Lars and I'm from Germany. I'm doing a summer course in Oxford and I'm er very lucky because my company – I work for an engineering company – is paying for it. I work in the foreign trade department. We sell machine parts to countries all over the world and I have to go to trade fairs and be able to communicate with people who speak different languages. I have to negotiate deals and also talk to people socially in restaurants and things like that. Sometimes I can use German but usually we speak English to our customers. In a way I think it's sad that English has become a *lingua franca* and that other languages, you know, are dying out because English is getting more important. But on the other hand, it's practical to have one language you can speak wherever you go. English is breaking down a lot of obstacles to communication. I suppose you can say that English doesn't belong to certain countries anymore. It's just everybody's world language.

P: My name's Paolo. I work in an export company in Brazil and I need English for my job, so I'm trying to improve it now. I love learning English. I spend all my free time trying to get better. I watch films in English and go to the pub and talk to people. It's really interesting to meet so many different people and just talk to them. I listen to a lot of music in English too. Often I can't understand the lyrics, but I like the sound of the language. I've got a bit of a problem with English as a *lingua franca*. I know English is important, at any rate you can't get by without it nowadays, but I sort of think it would be better if everybody learnt more foreign languages. Native speakers of English are quite arrogant. They think they don't need to speak anybody else's language. They're kind of imposing their way of life and their view of the world on other people through their language, and a lot of people oppose that.

Unit 3 Net value

Listening script 05

Some people think the Internet is a good thing.

The most powerful educational tool the world has ever known.

It's preserving our history, making sure that in the future we never forget the past.

The Internet is a place that is free from state intervention, censorship, and control. The only place where freedom of speech truly exists.

Orwell was wrong. It is not the state that holds all the power. It is us.

Some people think the Internet is a good thing. What do you think?

Some people think the Internet is a bad thing.

Somewhere your identity can be stolen, your home invaded and your savings robbed without anyone setting foot inside your door.

It is one of the most dangerous weapons ever created. A way for the unhinged to spread evil, free of supervision or censorship. A place for mankind to exercise its darkest desires. An open market where you can purchase anything you want.

Orwell was right. The Internet has taken us to a place where everything we do is watched, monitored and processed without us ever realising.

Some people think the Internet is a bad thing. What do you think?

Listening script 06

(G = Graham, L = Layla)

G: Have you seen those ads for the Internet? You know the ones about whether the Internet is a good or bad thing?

L: Oh yeah, they're clever, very dramatic. They really get the message across.

G: Yes, they are good, but I couldn't figure out what it was all about at first. Isn't it a bit strange for an internet company to be questioning its own product?

L: They've got everybody talking, though … I think most people will say the Internet is a good thing – on balance. All that information and stuff, and it's free! The Internet's, like, a part of life now. I can't imagine not having the Internet for downloading music, shopping and whatever.

G: Yeah, there's lots of information, as you point out, but how much of that is useable? The Net's like a huge rubbish dump, anybody can chuck things in there. You can search forever and you never know how accurate things are, things disappear as soon as they're not news … and what do you mean by 'it's free'? All the articles I've tried to access recently had to be paid for. Give me a decent library any day!

L: So in other words, you'd rather live in the good old days. Come off it!

G: Well, what about credit card fraud and identity theft and that sort of thing? Do you know what I mean? Don't you worry about things like that?

L: Not really, if people want to er … if they want to take you for a ride, they'll always find a way, they don't need the Internet to do it. What it boils down to is being careful. You can't stop using something because it has a couple of risks.

G: Yeah, fair enough but er … so you're not really bothered about the risks?

L: No, what I'm getting at is that, it isn't an open-and-shut case but the pros definitely outweigh the cons.

G: I'm not sure you're right there. I mean you were on about music and shopping. Yeah, great, but there are so many other aspects. Information equals power nowadays, it's the key to everything – information society and all that … Are you with me?

Most of the Internet is dominated by English-speaking websites and American companies. I think I read that 75% or so of websites are in English and so …

L: Not true. It's 50%, or 50-ish, anyway. People are waking up to the fact that customers want websites in their own language … And the Internet actually helps countries that … er, countries with few resources because it gives them, you know, a kind of platform to make their problems known, and that, well that can lead to increased cooperation and tolerance between countries.

G: Yeah, that's the rose-tinted view, the Internet strengthens social bonds and all that … But the reality is the Net alienates people. What I mean is, look at how many people send emails instead of using the phone. It's so impersonal.

L: Ah, but you can always telephone over the Internet with video, that's even better than the phone!

G: OK, OK … why did I start this?

Listening script 07

Speaking and pronunciation Ex 3 from page 75

Listening script 08

Reading text from page 77

Unit 4 Team spirit

Listening script 09

Reading text from page 79

Listening script 10

(L = Liz, M = Maria, E = Ethan)

L: Hello and welcome to *Dear Liz*. I'm Liz Cooper, here to help you with all your work problems. Today our topic is difficult colleagues. And our first caller is already on the line. Maria. Hello, Maria. What's your problem?

M: Er well, I started working at an advertising agency a few months ago – it's my first job and I really like the work. The problem is that I work with someone who is always really rude when I ask a question or make a suggestion. Her whole attitude is one of non-cooperation and I've had enough of it.

L: Is this person part of your team?

M: Yes – theoretically anyway. In reality she seems to think her ideas are the best and she completely ignores whatever ideas I put forward. I'm tired of all the friction. It's really getting me down.

L: Hmm, yes, I can see your difficulty. What's interesting is that difficult people rarely see themselves as the difficult one. If you're willing to talk with this person – and I think you should do so – then it's a good idea to consider an approach that won't put your colleague on the defensive.

M: What do you mean?

L: Well, first of all talking away from your work environment might help. And rather than making assumptions or placing blame, I recommend you begin the conversation by asking questions. Ask about ways you may be contributing to the problems you've identified. Perhaps you make too many suggestions or ask questions in a manner that seems impertinent from someone who is new to the company.

M: Mmm, OK, well, I'll give it a try. Thank you.

L: You're welcome, good luck Maria. … Right, on the line now is Ethan. Hi Ethan, how can I help?

E: Hi Liz, well, I'm a student and I work at a call centre at weekends to pay for my studies. Anyway, I'd like your advice on a problem with my new supervisor. She's determined to make my life a misery.

L: What does she do exactly?

E: Well, she talks down to me and she constantly has to know my whereabouts and what I'm doing. I think she's out of order.

L: So you haven't had this problem with other supervisors?

E: Never. It's put me in a real dilemma. I can't afford to leave because like I said, I need the money for my course but I can't stand working there now.

L: Have you tried approaching your colleague directly?

E: No, I haven't. To tell the truth I'm a bit scared of her and I don't want to cause a scene.

L: Hmm, but as long as you fear her, you surrender to her. When you're not afraid of her, the dynamics of your relationship will change. Stand up to her.

E: Right, but how do I do that?

L: My advice is, speak to her and ask her about the issues she has with you. You don't have to meet with her alone; ask her manager or someone from the personnel department to be present. Then if nothing changes you should think about going to the company's legal department.

E: OK, thank you for your advice.

L: Thank you for calling. Ethan. …

Unit 5 Review

Listening script 11

(P = Presenter, AW = Professor Alistair Watson)

P: A recent survey conducted by psychologists at various universities in the UK and the US has found that a person's taste in music, and how it's organised, may help predict which personality groups he or she belongs to, and that if you want to assess a person's character, a quick look through their music collection is one of the most reliable ways of doing so. With me here today to tell us more is Professor Alistair Watson. Professor Watson.

AW: Hello. Around 5,000 volunteers participated in the research. And, yes, it does seem that taste in music does, broadly speaking, correlate with a person's personality.

P: And how was the research carried out?

AW: The key element was getting the volunteers to create a 10-track CD of their favourite songs. Strangers then judged what the anonymous compilers were like. We found that the CD assessment proved significantly more reliable than any other ways of quickly assessing people such as by looks, clothes, taste in films, and so on. For example, people who listen to classical music are more likely to be, and be seen as, quite reflective, and generally very well-read and knowledgeable people. Looking at more contemporary music, pop and chart music fans tend to be quite straightforward and conventional – they're generally pretty dutiful and reliable sort of people. Whereas rap and hip-hop fans, on the other hand, are likely to be a bit more, let's say, socially liberal, rebellious and more image-conscious.

P: So, do we know why musical likes and dislikes are so closely linked to personality?

AW: Well, it seems there's much more to listening to music than, well, just enjoying it. It's thought that individuals select music to send out signals to establish how they like to be seen. For some, music can be central to their way of life, and is why they dress, have their hair and generally look the way they do.

P: But isn't that, particularly with younger people, just a way of asserting your identity?

AW: Well, to a certain extent, yes, I think it is. But at the same time, and as we were saying, a person's musical likes and dislikes can reveal a lot more about a person.

Listening script 12

(P = Presenter, AW = Professor Alistair Watson)

P: … And you also found that how a person organises their music is a reflection of their personality.

AW: Yes. People organise their CDs and MP3 files in different ways and this certainly indicates personality types. Some are alphabeticised or divided into genre and so on, or, and this is much more common we found, more randomly arranged. If your CDs are stored in no particular order then you are probably more artistic and open to new experiences and ideas. The opposite - religiously following a strict organisational formula – is a sign of an obsessive-compulsive personality. One of the volunteers in the research springs to mind. She and her fiancé live together and they have a sort of music room, which has two walls totally filled with shelves of CDs. I think they must have about a thousand between them, or thereabouts. Her CDs are very carefully organised by genre and then within this by artist and then alphabeticised yet again by album title within that. Now, she is clearly an extremely organised and reliable person, the kind who doesn't get parking tickets and that sort of thing. But what is really quite interesting is that she and her boyfriend, and I think they've been together for a couple of years now, have not yet combined their collections. Why they haven't done so, I don't know. His CDs are stacked completely randomly, by the way.

P: Mmm, maybe it would be interesting to follow that up – see where they, and their CDs, are in another two years or so. And I understand that some of the research looked at how music plays a part in the way couples interact.

AW: Yes. We monitored 'new' couples' first six weeks of conversation, and discovered that they used music to 'check each other out' nearly twice as much as books, television, sport or whatever. Essentially, they were using music to communicate their character types.

P: So, next time you're trying to size somebody up, a quick look through their CD collection really does seem to be as good a place to start as any. Thank you Professor Watson.

Listening script 13

Song from page 84

Communication activities

Unit 2, Speaking and pronunciation Ex 3 page 73

1 Read your rolecard for both situations.
2 Prepare notes to help you with your roles.
3 Do the role-plays with Student A. Include the phrases in Speaking and pronunciation Ex 1 and some of the euphemisms from page 70.

Rolecard 1

Your friend was fired from his / her job a couple of months ago. He / she has been very depressed, staying at home eating fast food and watching TV. Now he / she looks terrible: pale, overweight and wearing dirty old clothes. You think your friend needs to hear the truth in order to pull himself / herself together and get on with life but given his / her emotional state, you need to tread softly.
Start like this: *Listen, I realise ...*

Rolecard 2

A close friend of yours has recently died and you are very upset. Student A is your flatmate. You have been having arguments with him / her the last couple of months about money – he / she looks after the finances and pays the bills and you feel you're always being asked for money. Now you think he / she is being unfair by talking about money at a time like this.

Unit 3, Reading and vocabulary Ex 3 page 77

Answers

1 two or three 2 an hour 3 41% 4 five
5 About a quarter 6 60% 7 About half (45%)
8 43%

Unit 4, Speaking Ex 2 page 81

Analysis

How did you score?

Mostly A's

You're a natural born leader just waiting for the right job to come along. You're strong, decisive, and authoritarian. Everyone around you respects you. At least that's what you'd like to think. In reality, the situation may be rather different. At best your arrogant, autocratic approach is seen as old fashioned. You would be wise to be less punitive to those who do not see the world as you do, and open up more to the talents of those around you.

Mostly B's

You've got good potential. You support people. You listen to others. You take the initiative. All this means you have a good professional future. But only if you overcome what could become a fatal career flaw – wanting to be liked. There is nothing wrong with seeking the approval of others, but you do this to such an extent that you want to be everyone's best friend. Try to learn to confront potential conflicts with sensitivity and honesty – people will respect you more for it.

Mostly C's

Management, here you come! You're creative, assertive and empathetic. You easily draw groups together and enjoy heading them up. Most promising, though, is the importance you give to bringing on the abilities of others. You have high expectations of them, higher possibly than they have of themselves. And you seem prepared to do what you can to help them realise their own potential. Be mindful, however, not to let more superficially forceful characters conquer your position.

Mostly D's

You're smart enough to have figured out by now that your place is more likely to be in, rather than at the head of, the team. You prefer to listen to ideas, not voice them. You prefer to implement decisions rather than make them. You're a solid, reliable, loyal team player. But be cautious that in your acquiescence to others, you don't become sycophantic. At times, be prepared to do things your own way.